SPICY AND DELICIOUS

Priya Wickramasinghe was born in Sri
Lanka. Since 1966, she and her husband, a
Professor of Astronomy, have lived in
England with their children, first in
Cambridge and now in Wales. In the
intervening years her passionate interest in
the spices and flavours of Far Eastern
cookery has grown rather than diminished,
and she now enjoys an international
reputation for her cuisine.

Spicy and Delicious

**Exotic and tasty recipes
from India and Sri Lanka**

Priya
Wickramasinghe

CORONET BOOKS
Hodder and Stoughton

Copyright © 1979 Priya Wickramasinghe

First published in Great Britain 1979 by
J. M. Dent & Sons Ltd.

Coronet edition 1981

British Library C.I.P.

Wickramasinghe, Priya
  Spicy and delicious.
  1. Cookery, Indic
  2. Cookery, Sri Lankan
  I. Title
  641.5954   TX724.5.I4

  ISBN 0 340 26676 7

Printed and bound in Great Britain for
Hodder and Stoughton Paperbacks, a
division of Hodder and Stoughton Ltd.,
Mill Road, Dunton Green, Sevenoaks,
Kent (Editorial Office: 47 Bedford
Square, London, WC1 3DP) by
Collins, Glasgow. Photoset by
Rowland Phototypesetting Ltd.,
Bury St Edmunds, Suffolk.

Contents

Introduction	7
Dictionary of Spices	13
Utensils and Serving	19
Basic Recipes	21
Rice and Bread	25
Meat, Poultry and Fish	39
Vegetables and Lentils	67
Salads and Chutneys	93
Savoury Treats and Side-dishes	103
Desserts and Sweets	117
Menu Suggestions	137
Appendix	141
Index	143

Introduction

The mystic Orient has an irresistible attraction – no less for the gastronomic adventurer than for the tourist, the naturalist and the sun-bather. The once-distant regions of the Indian subcontinent and Sri Lanka are now accessible to tourists from the West who are enticed there by pictures of palm-fringed beaches, spectacular ancient temples and monuments and the promise of relaxation amidst a culture that is over 2500 years old. Along with this easy accessibility has come a surge of interest in the culinary delights of these countries, and dishes from India and Sri Lanka are gradually gaining acceptance in the day-to-day repertoire of the Western cook. Curries are becoming synonymous with adventure, relaxation, even aphrodisia!

Within the Indian subcontinent itself there are many different ethnic and religious groups, and each separate group has its own distinctive culture as well as culinary style. Regional differences are also pronounced. Despite its proximity to India, Sri Lanka can in no way be regarded as an extension of the neighbouring sub-continent. Culturally, geographically, climatically and indeed gastronomically, the differences are marked. A distinctive 'Sri Lankan' identity pervades all facets of life on this beautiful tropical island.

Urban life in India and Sri Lanka has evolved over many centuries. The life-styles of the indigenous ethnic groups, already quite different from one another, have, over the centuries, been influenced by those of visiting

7

races – notably the trading Moors and the invading Europeans. Such interactions have led inevitably to the evolution of hybrid culinary styles, the result of a gradual assimilation of many different influences. The main aim of *Spicy and Delicious* is to bring this hybrid culinary experience within the reach of the Western palate. Well-tested and tried-out recipes are introduced here. All these have been prepared using ingredients which are readily available in Great Britain, the United States, Canada and Australia. And invariably the results have been ecstatically received!

India and Sri Lanka together cover a large area of the globe, and the geographical and climatic variations across their terrain are considerable. Most of this land mass lies within the tropical belt and produces an abundance of exotic tropical fruits, vegetables and pulses of all kinds. Rice is the staple food in South India and Sri Lanka, and wheat is the stable diet in North India. The spices which give Indian and Sri Lankan food its distinctive flavour and character are grown throughout the area. Not only are the types of spices relevant, but the blending of one spice with another produces important differences in the culinary styles of the various regions of the Indian subcontinent and Sri Lanka.

For many centuries nations fought for the monopoly of the relatively small areas of the Earth's surface where spices grew abundantly. The history of India and Sri Lanka is intimately connected with the course of such international squabbles. In the 16th century the Portuguese were the first of the Europeans to discover in Sri Lanka and in parts of India a rich source of cinnamon, cardamom, cloves and nutmeg – spices which play a crucial role in all Indian and Sri Lankan cookery – and which were originally used, both in the East and the West, for their preservative properties. Only much later were spices used for their flavour and fragrance and for garnishing.

Cinnamon, cardamom, nutmeg, coriander and chilli are still extensively cultivated throughout the Indian subcontinent and are the main ingredients of curry powder which plays such an important part in Indian and Sri Lankan cooking. To make a curry powder each of these spices is ground separately into a fine powder and these are then mixed together in varying proportions depending on the dish for which they are required. The hotness of a curry depends upon the quantity used of only one of the ingredients – chilli. The amount of it used can be varied according to individual taste and, for those with an aversion to hot food, can even be entirely omitted without undue sacrifice. Ground dried red chilli powder is available from Indian and Chinese grocery stores, along with all the other spices included in the recipes. Ready-mixed curry powders are no substitute for individual blending. This is particularly so because vegetables, pulses, fish and meat all require different spices mixed in differing proportions.

Because the staple food of a large part of India and Sri Lanka is rice, a rice dish invariably forms the pivot of the main course, giving both bulk and body to a meal. Fish, meat and vegetable curries and salads are arranged, often artistically, around a rice dish. There are many varieties of rice and also many different ways in which the grain is processed before it reaches the grocery store. Not all types of rice which are available on the market are suitable for curries. Basmati rice, available in all Indian shops, is undoubtedly the best. But if this is difficult to obtain, any long grain patna rice or patna-type rice will suffice.

There is no mystique about making good boiled rice. The following prescription should ensure an excellent result. The rice should first be washed in a large strainer or colander under running cold water until the water runs clear. Two cups of water are then added to every one cup of rice in the pan. This is now rapidly brought

9

to the boil, lid open. When it comes to the boil the heat is reduced so as to just simmer, the pan is covered and the cooking time from this stage is precisely fifteen minutes. On no account should the lid be opened for inspection during this time. You should get perfect fluffy rice with grains well separated and the water fully absorbed.

Coconut has a multitude of culinary uses. Those slender leaning coconut palm trees that adorn tropical beaches provide one of the most important crops in South India and Sri Lanka. Nothing is wasted from a coconut tree. A cool refreshing drink is obtained from the golden-yellow young nuts, and the kernel is eaten. For curries the kernel of the mature nut is scraped out and the rich milk extracted. The scraped kernel is used for salads (sambols) and chutneys. Solidified coconut milk is marketed in the form of slabs called 'Cream of Coconut', available in all Indian grocery stores. Kernel scrapings are available in the form of desiccated coconut (unsweetened) in most supermarkets and grocery stores. Coconut oil is frequently used as a frying agent in cooking, but any vegetable oil such as sunflower oil or corn oil will do just as well.

Other coconut products include toddy and jaggery. Toddy is an alcoholic beverage produced from the sweet sap of the palm. Distilled, toddy gives the hard liquor known as arrack. The sap from palm flowers is also used to make jaggery, the sweetening agent used in many Indian and Sri Lankan desserts. This is also available in Indian shops throughout Great Britain, the United States, Canada and Australia.

The truly indigenous diet of the people of the Indian subcontinent was probably exclusively vegetarian. The climatic conditions which prevail in India and Sri Lanka make for an abundance of pulses and a wide variety of vegetables, ranging from distinctly tropical vegetables to those which grow in temperate climes. In the hill country of Sri Lanka, for instance, all the familiar English vegetables such as cabbage, cauliflower and carrots grow well. In the hotter lowland regions all manner of exotic tropical vegetables can be grown. For each vegetable there is a particular way of preparation, and a particular array of spices best suited to bring out its flavour. It should be remembered that at least three separate vegetable dishes usually accompany each main course of an Indian or Sri Lankan meal.

The best delicatessen stores and Indian and Chinese food stores in all major European and American cities stock a variety of tropical vegetables and pulses. These include aubergines, bhindi (okra), white radish, karella, coriander leaves, sweet potatoes and lentils. Lentils provide an important source of protein and vitamins, particularly in a vegetarian diet, and there are several types on the market, each with a distinctive colour, size and flavour. These include masur dhal, moong dhal, urad dhal and chana, to name but a few. Some types of lentil are ground into flour (commercially referred to as gram flour), and this flour is used instead of refined wheat flour or wholewheat flour for thickening gravies, making lentil flour pancakes, and so on. The recipes in this book are confined to those vegetables and lentils that are readily available in the West.

Meat is such a rarity as to be a luxury in many parts of India and Sri Lanka. But despite this there is a wide variety of recipes for meat and poultry dishes, which are eaten mainly by the higher income groups. Not surprisingly fishing is an important cottage industry in coastal areas, and a good deal of fish is included in the normal diet of the inhabitants of the Indian coastal cities and of Sri Lanka. There are many different ways in which they use fish in cooking. Dried, powdered fish is often used for seasoning curries, along with spices; and, of course, fish, shrimp and crab make delicious curries!

11

Dictionary of Spices

Spices are used for flavouring and garnishing the cuisine of most countries of the world, but nowhere are they used as extensively and as imaginatively as they are in the Indian subcontinent. They are used in curries as well as in rice preparations, in savoury dishes as well as in sweets. Since the range of spices commonly used in Western dishes is small, a list of spices that will be needed and their uses and properties is given below:

Allspice

Partly dried berries of *Pimenta dioica*, a tropical tree of the myrtle family. Allspice is, in fact, used more in Western cooking than in Indian cuisine. It owes its name to the belief that it combines the flavours of cinnamon, cloves and nutmeg.

Aniseed

This spice is widely grown throughout Asia and is used in curries in a roasted form. It is a seed derived from the herb *Pimpinella anisum*.

Asafoetida

This pungently smelling resin is obtained from the root of the herb *Ferula foetida*. It is cultivated widely in the Middle East and it is used in many vegetable dishes.

Capsicum

Also called sweet pepper, this is used for curries, but it is not hot or pungent like chilli.

Caraway

These are black seeds derived from the herb *Carum carvi* which have a distinctive flavour resembling slightly the flavour of aniseed. It is not very frequently used in curries.

Cardamom

These are the dried seeds of *Elettaria cardamomum*, a herb of the ginger family. Whole cardamom pods are used for flavouring rice, but these should be removed before serving. For curries the seeds are removed from the pods and ground. In some parts of India cardamoms are used for flavouring tea and coffee. It is also chewed after meals as a breath-sweetener.

Cayenne Pepper

This is made by grinding the dried pods and seeds of *Capsicum frutescens* to a fine powder. It is darker than paprika and very much hotter. Cayenne pepper is a good substitute for chilli.

Chilli

This is a small, very hot variety of capsicum (*Capsicum annum*) which can be either red or green. Dried red pods are used whole or are ground to make chilli powder. Either whole chillies or chilli powder can be used in curries. This single ingredient is responsible for the hotness of curries.

Cinnamon

This fragrant spice is the dried bark of *Cinnamomum zeylanicum*, grown mainly in Sri Lanka. It is an important ingredient of curries, and it is also used in sweet dishes.

Cloves

These dried unopened flower buds of *Eugenia caryophyllata* or *Myrtus caryophyllus* are another major ingredient in Indian and Sri Lankan cooking. Cloves have been an important commodity in the spice trade.

Coriander (*Coriandrum sativum*)

Its leaves are used for garnishing dishes and the crushed seeds are used in curry powder.

Cumin

The seeds of black cumin (*Cuminum nigrum*) and white cumin (*Cuminum cyminum*) are ground and used in many sweet and savoury dishes.

Curry Leaves

The leaves of *Murraya koenigii*, a small shrub of the orange family, are often used in curries, particularly in South India and Sri Lanka. They add a characteristic fragrance and flavour.

Fennel

This herb is thought to be one of the oldest used by man. Ground seeds of *Foeniculum vulgare* or *Nigella sativa* are used in curries. Fresh or dried seeds are also chewed after a meal as a digestive or breath-sweetener.

Fenugreek

This spice is derived from the aromatic seeds of the plant *Trigonella Foencum graecum*. Roasted, ground fenugreek seeds are used in curry powder.

Garam Masala

This is the name given to a mixture of spices used for curries. Commercially-mixed garam masala is obtainable from Indian grocery stores. Recipes for making your own garam masala from individual spices are given in Basic Recipes.

Ginger

This is the root of the herbaceous plant *Zingiber officinales* which is used extensively in Indian and Sri Lankan cooking. Fresh ginger (called 'green' ginger) is to be preferred to dried ginger powder.

Jaggery

This sweetening agent, obtained from various types of palm, is used for making many Sri Lankan desserts.

Mace

The lacy outer covering of the nutmeg (see below).

Maldive Fish

Dried fish from the Maldive Islands is used in many Sri Lankan curries. It is sold in Indian grocery stores.

Mustard seed

The small dark-brown seed of *Brassica juncea* is used whole and fried in hot oil in the preparation of most curries. Mustard oil is also used in cooking, particularly in Bengal.

Nutmeg

The seed of the evergreen tree, known as *Myristica fragrans*. Grated nutmeg is used both in curries and in sweet dishes. Nutmeg is grown in Sri Lanka and throughout the Malay archipelago.

Pepper (Piper nigrum)

This most familiar spice comes from a vine which is native to Sri Lanka, South India and Malaya. Dried berries become peppercorns, which can be ground.

Poppy Seeds

Seeds of the opium poppy (*Papaver somniferum*) are often added to curry powders. They have no smell, but have a nutty flavour. They are believed to stimulate the appetite!

Saffron

The dried stamen of *Crocus sativus* is one of the most expensive of spices. Saffron gives a dish a delicate aroma and a golden-yellow colour. A very minute quantity (a few stamens or ¼ teaspoonful of powder) goes a long way.

Sesame Seed

Seeds from the herbaceous plant *Sesamum indicum* are extensively used in Indian cooking. Oil from this seed is called gingerly oil and is used for frying. The powdered seeds are often mixed into curry powders.

Tamarind

The dried fruit of the Tamarind tree (*Tamarindus indica*) can be soaked in hot water to extract its tart acidic juice. This extract is then used for cooking curry dishes.

Turmeric

The root of *Curcuma longa*, a perennial herb, is dried and then ground into a powder. This brilliant yellow-coloured powder is used as a flavouring and colouring in curries.

Utensils and Serving

The equipment used in a traditional Indian or Sri Lankan kitchen is rudimentary, even primitive. Meals are cooked in earthenware pots on an open brick stove. The grinding of spices and condiments is done using a mortar and pestle or a grinding stone. Although modern technology has inevitably changed some of the equipment used in Oriental kitchens, basic methods of cooking have not significantly changed. The average Western kitchen will be suitably equipped for cooking all the dishes that I shall describe. For cooking on gas or electric stoves I have found it preferable to use heavy-bottomed pans. But when tamarind or vinegar is used metal receptacles, especially pans made of copper, should be avoided. For use in cooking wooden spoons are always better than metal spoons, but it is wise to set aside separate wooden spoons for savoury and sweet dishes. An electric coffee grinder is an excellent modern substitute for a mortar and pestle for grinding spices. A large sieve will come in handy for many of the procedures that I shall describe.

Most Indian and Sri Lankan dishes do not require much in the way of garnishing. The commonly used garnishes are finely chopped coriander leaves, crisply fried sliced onion and chopped nuts. The traditional way of serving Indian food is on a large silver or stainless steel circular plate known as a *thali*.

Several smaller silver bowls containing curries of

various kinds are arranged on the periphery of the *thali*. Rice or bread is served at the centre of the *thali*. Pickles, chutneys and sweetmeats are also served on the *thali* itself. In Sri Lanka meals are served in Western-style dishes. A typical meal would consist of a main rice or bread dish, three or four different vegetable curries, a fish or meat curry and a selection of pickles, chutneys and sweetmeats.

Basic Recipes

For many Indian curries a basic curry powder mix known as garam masala is augmented with individual spices used in varying proportions. Ready-mixed garam masala is available in most Indian grocery stores and is perfectly acceptable as a basic mix. However, you might prefer to make your own mix and there are several tested recipes to choose from. I give here four recipes that I have found quite satisfactory.

Recipes for Garam Masala (Curry Powder)

Recipe 1

2 tablespoonfuls coriander seed
2 tablespoonfuls cumin seed
1 teaspoonful each of fenugreek, mustard and poppy seed
2 teaspoonfuls each of cardamom seed, cloves and dry red chilli
1 tablespoonful black peppercorns
1 tablespoonful ground turmeric
1 tablespoonful ground ginger

Grind all the seeds in a coffee grinder. Add the turmeric and then mix with the ground ginger. Store in an airtight jar.

Recipe 2

4 tablespoonfuls coriander seed
1 tablespoonful cumin seed
½ tablespoonful ground cinnamon
1 teaspoonful cardamom seed
1 teaspoonful cloves
1 teaspoonful nutmeg
1 teaspoonful black peppercorns
½ teaspoonful ground mace

Roast all the ingredients in a heavy-bottomed pan for about 10 minutes. Allow to cool. Grind all the cooked ingredients in a coffee grinder. Store in an airtight jar.

Recipe 3

3 tablespoonfuls coriander seed
3 tablespoonfuls cumin seed
3 tablespoonfuls black peppercorns
1 tablespoonful cardamom seed
2 teaspoonfuls ground cloves
1 tablespoonful ground cinnamon
2 teaspoonfuls ground mace

Grind all the ingredients in a coffee grinder. Store in an airtight container.

Recipe 4

4 tablespoonfuls ground coriander
2 tablespoonfuls ground cumin
1 tablespoonful ground fennel
1 teaspoonful ground turmeric
1 teaspoonful ground cinnamon
1 teaspoonful ground cloves
1 teaspoonful ground cardamom
½ teaspoonful ground fenugreek
1 teaspoonful ground black pepper

Mix thoroughly. Store in an airtight container.

Ghee or Clarified Butter

8 oz (226 gm) unsalted butter

In a heavy-bottomed pan heat the butter on a very low heat for about 30 minutes. Remove the floating scum. Strain through a muslin into a bowl and allow to cool. Keep in a refrigerator. Use instead of butter or oil.

Pot of Tea

In Sri Lanka and India a meal would not be complete without a cup of tea. Tea is the major highland crop, particularly in Sri Lanka, and the gentle fragrance of tea pervades the cool hill-country air. In my opinion the best teas are the most fragrant and delicately flavoured ones which come from the highlands of Sri Lanka. Any specialist food store would stock Ceylon or Sri Lankan tea. Ask for a good quality high-grown Broken Orange Pekoe Ceylon tea and follow these instructions.

Take a tea pot (preferably a china pot) to a kettle of boiling water. Warm the pot by adding a little boiling water to the teapot, swishing it around and pouring out. Add tea leaves to the pot – one teaspoonful per person (cup) and one for the pot – then the freshly boiling water and stir. Replace lid and allow to stand for 3 minutes. Strain into cups and serve with milk and sugar.

If you have a sweet tooth try serving the tea with a teaspoonful of sweetened condensed milk per cup and sugar to taste. This is a popular way of serving tea in Sri Lanka. The condensed milk imparts a distinctive flavour.

Rice and Bread

Rice

(Serves 3–4)

8 oz (226 gm) rice (washed in a sieve under running cold
  water until the water runs clear)
20 fl oz (568 ml) water
½ teaspoonful salt

Put rice, water and salt in a saucepan and bring to the
boil. Stir, cover and simmer for 15 minutes. It is vital
that the lid should be kept on for the full 15 minutes.

Pilaf Rice

(Serves 3–4)

2 tablespoonfuls butter, ghee (see receipe on p. 23) or oil
1 medium-sized onion finely chopped
8 oz (226 gm) rice (washed in a sieve under running cold
  water and left to drain)
½ teaspoonful salt
6 cardamoms, 6 cloves and 1-in. (2·5-cm) stick of cinnamon
a few curry leaves (optional)
20 fl oz (568 ml) water
1 chicken stock cube

Heat the fat in a saucepan and brown the onion in it.
Add all the other ingredients (except the stock cube and

water) and fry over a gentle heat for 5 minutes. Lastly add the water in which the stock cube has been dissolved and bring to a rapid boil. Stir, cover and simmer for 15 minutes.

Optional variation – add 4 oz (113 gm) finely sliced fried mushrooms for garnish.

Vegetable Pilaf (Serves 3–4)

2 tablespoonfuls ghee or butter or oil
1 medium-sized onion chopped
1 small carrot grated
1 leek washed and finely sliced
4 oz (113 gm) peas (frozen or fresh)
1 teaspoonful salt
8 oz (226 gm) rice (washed in a sieve under running cold water)
20 fl oz (568 ml) water

Heat fat and fry onion. Add all the vegetables and stir over a low heat for a few minutes. Lastly add the rice and the water and boil. Cover and simmer for 15 minutes. Garnish with sliced hard-boiled eggs and tomato slices.

Vegetable Biriani   (Serves 4)

8 oz (226 gm) rice (washed in a sieve under running cold
water and left to drain)
20 fl oz (568 ml) water
1 teaspoonful salt
8 oz (226 gm) aubergines
8 oz (226 gm) onions
4 oz (113 gm) green pepper chopped
8 oz (226 gm) firm ripe tomatoes chopped
20 fl oz (568 ml) cooking oil

Put the rice, water and salt in a pan and bring to the
boil. Stir, cover and simmer for 15 minutes. While the
rice is cooking dice and deep fry the aubergines. Finely
slice the onions and fry until golden brown and leave to
drain.

Using a 4-pint casserole assemble all the ingredients
in layers starting and finishing with the rice. Cover with
a well-fitting lid and bake at gas mark 3 (320° F) for
30 minutes. (10 fl oz (284 ml) of double cream poured
over the top makes an interesting change.)

Left-over cold meat may be added to make a nourishing
'all in one' dish.

Lentil Rice   (Serves 4)

4 oz (113 gm) yellow moong or Masur dhal
4 oz (113 gm) rice
1 medium-sized onion sliced
2 tablespoonfuls oil
½ teaspoonful salt
½ teaspoonful ground turmeric
20 fl oz (568 ml) hot water
½ teaspoonful ground cumin
¼ teaspoonful mustard seed
a few curry leaves

Wash the lentils and soak them in water for 2 hours.
Wash rice and drain lentils and rice in a sieve. Heat oil
and fry onion until lightly brown. Add rice and lentils
and fry over a low heat for about 5 minutes. Add all the
other ingredients and bring to the boil. Cover and
simmer for 15 minutes.

Coconut Milk Rice (Yellow Rice)

2 tablespoonfuls ghee, butter or oil
½ medium-sized onion finely chopped
8 oz (226 gm) rice (washed in a sieve under running cold
   water and left to drain)
a few curry leaves
3 cloves
3 cardamom pods
1-in. (2·5-cm) stick cinnamon
1 teaspoonful salt
¼ teaspoonful ground saffron or turmeric
8 black peppercorns
20 fl oz (568 ml) boiling water in which 2 oz (56 gm)
   creamed coconut has been dissolved

Fry the finely chopped onion in the oil. Add all the other dry ingredients and fry over a low heat until the grains of rice become pale brown. Add the creamed coconut and water and bring to a rapid boil. Cover and simmer for 15 minutes.

This is a rice dish made for festive occasions in Sri Lanka.

Spicy Risotto

8 oz (226 gm) basmati rice
1½ fl oz (42 ml) oil
1 medium-sized onion finely chopped
2 medium-sized carrots grated
½ green pepper chopped
8 oz (226 gm) cooked meat (lamb, pork or chicken) cut into
   small pieces
1 teaspoonful salt
4 oz (113 gm) frozen peas
⅛ teaspoonful ground cardamom
¼ teaspoonful ground cinnamon
¼ teaspoonful ground cloves
20 fl oz (568 ml) hot water

Wash the rice in a sieve and allow to drain. Heat the oil
and fry the onion until lightly browned. Add the rice
and fry for about 5 minutes on a low heat. Add the rest
of the ingredients and bring rapidly to the boil. Reduce
the heat to a minimum and cook covered for 15 minutes.

This is an ideal way of using the left-over meat from a
Sunday joint. When served with a green salad it provides a balanced meal.

Chicken Biriani

¼ teaspoonful ground cumin
¼ teaspoonful ground coriander
½ teaspoonful paprika
¼ teaspoonful ground turmeric
8 cloves
seeds of 8 cardamom pods
½ teaspoonful ground cinnamon
1 green chilli (optional)
1 medium-sized onion
3 cloves garlic
1 teaspoonful finely chopped ginger
½ teaspoonful tomato puree
1 teaspoonful salt
5 fl oz (142 ml) yoghurt
1 lb (454 gm) de-boned fresh chicken

Blend all the above ingredients, except the chicken, in a liquidizer. Cut the chicken into bite-sized pieces. Marinade the chicken in the spicy yoghurt mixture for at least 4 hours.

For the rice one needs:

1 tablespoonful ghee, butter or oil
½ medium-sized onion finely chopped
12 oz (339 gm) rice washed and drained in a sieve
15 fl oz (426 ml) hot water
1 chicken stock cube
1 teaspoonful salt

Heat the oil and fry the onion until golden brown. Add the rice and fry over a low heat until the grains are translucent. Add the water in which the stock cube has been dissolved and bring to the boil. Cover and simmer for 10 minutes.

While the rice is cooking heat a tablespoonful of oil and quickly fry the chicken in it. Pour in the marinade and simmer for about 5 minutes.

Use a large casserole dish and place ⅓ of the rice at the bottom. Put half the chicken over the rice and cover with ⅓ of the rice. Put in the remainder of the chicken and cover it with the rest of the rice. Measure the marinade liquid and if it is less than 10 fl oz (284 ml) add hot water to make it up to this amount. Dissolve ¼ teaspoonful of saffron in the marinade liquid and pour it over the casserole. Bake covered at gas mark 3 (325° F) for 45 minutes.

Garnish with about 2 oz (56 gm) fried cashew-nuts and 8 oz (226 gm) finely sliced onions which have been deep fried until golden brown.

Serve with pickle and chutney.

Savoury Rice Sticks (String Hopper Pulao) (Serves 4)

8 oz (226 gm) rice sticks (available at Indian or Chinese stores)
2 tablespoonfuls oil
½ medium-sized onion chopped
2 carrots grated
4 oz (113 gm) fresh or frozen peas
½ green pepper chopped
2 tablespoonfuls tomato ketchup
1 teaspoonful salt
2 tablespoonfuls water

In a large pan bring 40 fl oz (1·4 litres) water to the boil. Add the rice sticks. Bring rapidly to the boil. Let it boil for 5 minutes. Drain into a colander. Heat the oil and fry the onion in it. Add the carrots, peas, green pepper and the rest of the ingredients and fry for 2 minutes. Add the water and simmer on a very low heat for 5 minutes. Stir in the rice sticks and mix thoroughly.

Rice sticks are eaten in Sri Lankan homes a few times a week. They are called 'string hoppers' and are freshly made each time with roasted rice flour. Commercially manufactured rice sticks are not normally used.

Sweet Rice (Serves 6–8)

1 tablespoonful ghee
12 oz (339 gm) rice (washed in a sieve until the water runs clear)
4 cloves
8 cardamom pods
¼ teaspoonful ground saffron dissolved in a few drops of hot water
8 oz (226 gm) brown sugar
1 oz (28 gm) each of blanched almonds, cashew-nuts and pistachios
1 oz (28 gm) sultanas
1 tablespoonful rosewater

In a pan heat the ghee. Fry the rice until the grains are translucent. Add the spices, sugar and 30 fl oz (852 ml) of hot water and bring rapidly to the boil. Cover and simmer for 10 minutes. Add the rest of the ingredients and simmer for a further 5 minutes. A delicious sweet rice. The sugar can be omitted and the rice can be eaten with any curry.

Chappatis

(Serves 3–4)

4 oz (113 gm) wholewheat flour
4 oz (113 gm) plain white flour
1½ teaspoonfuls salt
5–6 fl oz (142–170 ml) tepid water

In a bowl mix the flour, salt and sufficient water to form a soft pliable dough. Knead the dough thoroughly and leave covered at room temperature for about 1 hour. Divide the dough into 10 equal portions. Dust each portion of dough generously with flour and roll out evenly to resemble a pancake.

Heat a griddle or a heavy bottomed frying pan. Turn on the grill to its maximum. Place the pancake of dough on the griddle and cook for 4 seconds. Turn over and allow to cook for 8 seconds, or until the chappati is lightly brown.

Now place the chappati on the grill (the browned side should be at the bottom). The chappati should puff up like a balloon. Prick with a fork to expel the hot air. Place on a plate and smear with butter or ghee.

Repeat process until all the chappatis are made. Chappatis should be cooked quickly on a fairly high heat, otherwise they tend to become hard and leathery. Serve with vegetables or meat. Chappatis can be substituted for bread.

Puri

(Serves 6–8)

4 oz (113 gm) wholewheat flour
4 oz (113 gm) plain white flour
1½ teaspoonfuls salt
2 teaspoonfuls oil
5–6 fl oz (142–170 ml) tepid water
oil for deep frying

In a bowl mix the flour, salt, oil and sufficient water to
form a soft pliable dough. Knead the dough thoroughly
and leave covered at room temperature for about 1
hour. A quantity of dough the size and shape of a
walnut is rolled to resemble a thin pancake about
2½–3 in. (6–8 cm) in diameter. This flattened dough is
then deep fried. Since it requires much skill to make
individual puris of perfect shape, I prefer to roll out
one-third of the mixed dough at a time into a large thin
pancake which I then cut into circles of about 2½–3 in.
(6–8 cm) in diameter. A pastry cutter or wine glass is
ideal.

The success of a puri is in its cooking. The oil should
be heated until it begins to smoke, and the puris should
be carefully immersed one at a time. After about 6
seconds in the hot oil the puri will begin to surface.
Using a frying spoon gently pat it down to keep it
submerged in the hot oil until it puffs up. Turn over and
allow to cook for a couple of seconds. This whole frying
process should take about 15–20 seconds per puri.

Puris are usually eaten with vegetables at the start of a
meal and are a great favourite among children and
adults alike.

Makes about 50.

Nan (Leavened Bread) (Serves 4)

6 fl oz (170 ml) water
½ teaspoonful sugar
1 oz (28 gm) dried yeast
1½ lb (680 gm) strong white flour
1 teaspoonful salt
10 fl oz (284 ml) natural yoghurt
4 tablespoonfuls melted ghee

Heat the water to 110° F ('hand hot') and stir in the sugar. Sprinkle the yeast and stir until dissolved. Allow to stand for 15–20 minutes in a warm place. Sieve the flour into a bowl. Add the salt to the flour. Make a well in the centre and gradually work in the yoghurt, the ghee and the yeast. Knead on a lightly floured board until smooth. Cover and keep in a warm place until double in size.

Punch down the dough and divide into 10 equal portions. Use the palms of your hands to flatten each portion of dough to resemble a fine pancake, oblong in shape. Leave on a greased baking tray for 30 minutes. Bake in a hot oven (gas mark 7, or 440° F) for 15 minutes.

Nan is the traditional accompaniment to Tandouri chicken. It is also eaten with vegetables by non-meat eaters.

Paratha
(Serves 4)

8 oz (226 gm) wholewheat flour
8 oz (226 gm) plain flour
1½ teaspoonfuls salt
5–6 fl oz (142–170 ml) tepid water
oil for shallow frying

In a bowl mix the flour, salt and sufficient water to form a soft pliable dough. Knead the dough thoroughly and leave covered at room temperature for about 1 hour.

Divide the dough into 10 equal portions. Roll each portion of dough to resemble a fine pancake. Using a pastry brush or the tips of your fingers rub some oil or ghee on half of the circular area and fold over. Rub oil again on half the area and fold over once more. Now you should have a piece of dough resembling a quarter of a circle or quadrant. Roll out the quadrant again to resemble a pancake.

Heat a tablespoonful of oil or ghee in a frying pan. Shallow fry each quadrant for about 4 minutes on each side, adding more oil as necessary. Serve with vegetables or meat.

Roti

(Serves 3)

8 oz (226 gm) plain flour
3 oz (85 gm) desiccated coconut
1 teaspoonful salt
5–6 fl oz (142–170 ml) water

In a bowl mix the flour, coconut and salt. Make a well in the centre and work in sufficient water to form a stiff dough. Knead thoroughly. Divide into 6 portions. On a greased surface using your fingers flatten out each portion to resemble an average-sized side plate. Heat a griddle or heavy-bottomed frying pan. Put in the roti and allow it to brown on each side.

This is a Sri Lankan breakfast dish and is eaten with a hot sambol. It is equally delicious with butter and jam.

Meat, Poultry and Fish

Beef Curry (Serves 3)

2 tablespoonfuls oil
1 medium-sized onion finely sliced
1 lb (454 gm) braising beef cut into 1-in. (2·5-cm) pieces
3 cloves garlic
1 teaspoonful finely chopped fresh ginger
¼ teaspoonful ground turmeric
2 teaspoonfuls malt vinegar
¼ teaspoonful freshly milled black pepper
1 teaspoonful salt
1½ teaspoonfuls ground coriander
1½ teaspoonfuls ground cumin
3 cardamoms
3 cloves ⎫ ground together
1-in. (2·5-cm) stick cinnamon ⎭
2 oz (56 gm) creamed coconut
4 fl oz (113 ml) water
1 teaspoonful chilli powder
¼ teaspoonful ground fenugreek

Heat the oil. Fry the onion until browned. Add the meat and fry over a low heat until quite brown. Add the spices and other ingredients and simmer for 1 hour.

Keema Curry

2 tablespoonfuls oil
1 medium-sized onion finely chopped
3 cloves garlic chopped
½ teaspoonful chopped fresh ginger
2 green chillies finely chopped
2 teaspoonfuls ground coriander
2 teaspoonfuls ground cumin
¼ teaspoonful ground turmeric
1 teaspoonful salt
1 teaspoonful garam masala
1 lb (454 gm) lean minced meat
1 teaspoonful tomato puree
2 oz (56 gm) creamed coconut
4 fl oz (113 ml) water
8 oz (226 gm) fresh or frozen peas

Heat oil and fry onion in it. Add the spices and fry for a few seconds. Add the meat and continue to fry over a low heat. Finally mix in the tomato puree, the creamed coconut and the water and allow to simmer for an hour. Toss in the peas and cook for a further 10 minutes.

Curried Meat Balls   (Serves 4)

1 thick slice stale bread soaked in 2½ fl oz (71 ml) water
1 lb (454 gm) minced meat
8 oz (226 gm) onions finely chopped
½ teaspoonful finely chopped fresh ginger
2 cloves garlic chopped
¼ teaspoonful freshly milled black pepper
1 teaspoonful garam masala
3 fl oz (85 ml) oil
8 oz (226 gm) potatoes cut into ½-in. (1-cm) cubes
1 teaspoonful ground coriander
1 teaspoonful ground cumin
a few curry leaves
½ teaspoonful salt
2 green chillies chopped
2 tablespoonfuls tomato puree
2 oz (56 gm) creamed coconut

Squeeze out the water from the bread and mix with the
mince, half the onions, the ginger, garlic, pepper and
garam masala. Shape into bite-size balls and place in a
greased tray and bake in the oven at gas mark 3 (325° F)
for 30 minutes.

While the meat is cooking prepare the sauce. Heat the
oil and fry the onions and potatoes in it. Add the spices,
the tomato puree and the creamed coconut dissolved in
2 fl oz (56 ml) hot water. When the sauce is boiling,
carefully add in the meat balls and the liquid from the
baking tray. Cook for about 20 minutes over a low heat.

Friccadels (Crisp-fried Meat Balls)

(Serves 4)

1 *thick slice of stale bread soaked in 2½ fl oz (71 ml) water*
1 *lb (454 gm) lean minced meat*
1 *medium-sized onion finely chopped*
2 *cloves of garlic minced or chopped*
1 *teaspoonful minced or chopped ginger*
1 *teaspoonful salt*
¼ *teaspoonful freshly milled black pepper*
2 *eggs*
oil for deep frying

Squeeze the water out of the bread. In a bowl mix all the ingredients thoroughly. Divide and shape into 20 balls. Beat 2 eggs and dip the meat balls into the egg and roll them in breadcrumbs. Heat the oil and deep fry the meat balls a few at a time for about 5 minutes. Drain on kitchen paper. Serve with rice or as an appetizer with drinks.

Nargisi Kofta

(Serves 2–3)

1 *lb 2 oz (509 gm) finely minced lamb or beef*
1 *tablespoonful chopped mint leaves*
1 *minced onion*
2 *cloves garlic crushed*
1 *teaspoonful garam masala*
1½ *teaspoonfuls salt*
¼ *teaspoonful freshly milled black pepper*
3 *eggs hard-boiled and shelled*
oil for deep frying

In a bowl mix the meat and the rest of the ingredients except the eggs. Divide the meat into 6 portions. Cut each egg lengthwise into two. Flatten a portion of the meat and place half an egg in the centre and cover with the meat, taking care to make sure that the egg is encased in the meat.

Heat the oil and over a low flame fry the kofta until evenly browned on all sides. Drain on paper. Serve with rice.

Chicken Curry (1)   (Serves 4)

2 tablespoonfuls oil
1 large onion finely sliced
1 teaspoonful chilli powder
¼ teaspoonful ground turmeric
4 cloves garlic crushed
1 teaspoonful finely chopped fresh ginger
a few curry leaves (optional)
1 tablespoonful coriander seed
1 tablespoonful cumin seed
6 peppercorns
4 cloves
3 cardamoms
1-in. (2·5-cm) piece of cinammon
1½ teaspoonfuls salt
4 chicken quarters weighing approximately 3 lb (1·3 kg),
   jointed
5 fl oz (142 ml) natural yoghurt
2 fl oz (56 ml) water

Heat the oil. Fry the onions until golden brown. Add all the spices except the yoghurt and fry for a few minutes. Cool the spices and grind in a blender. Heat another tablespoonful of oil and gently fry the pieces of chicken. Add the ground spices, the yoghurt and water, and simmer over a low heat for about 45 minutes. (Where time is limited instead of grinding the spices, ground cumin and coriander can be used. The pepper, cardamoms, cloves and cinnamon can be replaced by 1½ teaspoonfuls of garam masala.)

Chicken Curry (2) (Serves 4)

2 large onions
2 tablespoonfuls ground coriander
2 teaspoonfuls ground cumin
½ teaspoonful ground turmeric
1 teaspoonful chilli powder
2-in. (5-cm) stick cinnamon
¼ teaspoonful ground cardamom
5 cloves
½ teaspoonful crushed green ginger
4 cloves garlic finely chopped
2 teaspoonfuls salt
4 fl oz (113 ml) vegetable oil
1 3-lb (1·3-kg) chicken, jointed
2 oz (56 gm) creamed coconut
10 fl oz (284 ml) hot water
juice of 1 lemon
2 tablespoonfuls finely chopped coriander leaves

Grind one of the onions, and the spices and salt. Finely slice the second onion and fry in the heated oil until golden brown. Add ground ingredients and stir for 5–10 minutes. Now add the chicken and fry for another 5 minutes. Dissolve the creamed coconut in the hot water and add to the chicken. Bring to the boil – lower the heat and simmer for about 1 hour. Before serving add the lemon juice and garnish with the coriander leaves.

Chicken Curry (3)　　　　(Serves 2–3)

4 teaspoonfuls ground coriander
2 teaspoonfuls ground cumin
1 teaspoonful garam masala
¼ teaspoonful ground cinnamon
¼ teaspoonful cloves
¼ teaspoonful ground cardamom
¼ teaspoonful ground turmeric
½ teaspoonful ground fennel
1 teaspoonful chilli powder
3 tablespoonfuls oil
1 medium-sized onion finely chopped
3 chicken quarters (each cut into two)
1½ teaspoonfuls salt
1 teaspoonful chopped ginger
4 cloves garlic
1 teaspoonful tomato puree
6 fl oz (170 ml) water

In a heavy-bottomed pan roast the ground spices over a low heat for about 7 minutes. Heat the oil and fry the onion until golden brown. Add the chicken and fry until the skins are lightly browned. Add the ground spices, salt, ginger, garlic and tomato puree. Pour in the water and bring to the boil. Lower the heat and simmer for about 1 hour.

By roasting the spices the gravy takes on a rich dark brown hue. This adds an unusual flavour to the curry.

Chicken Kashmiri-style (Serves 4)

1 fresh chicken approximately 3½ lb (1·5 kg) in weight
2 tablespoonfuls ghee or oil
1 medium-sized onion finely chopped
1 teaspoonful ginger finely chopped
4 cloves garlic finely chopped
1 teaspoonful salt
½ teaspoonful ground cinnamon
½ teaspoonful ground coriander
½ teaspoonful ground cumin
¼ teaspoonful freshly milled black pepper
½ teaspoonful ground cloves
½ teaspoonful ground cardamom
1 chicken stock cube
5 fl oz (142 ml) water
4 oz (113 gm) ground almonds
4 oz (113 gm) ground pistachio
10 fl oz (284 ml) yoghurt
½ teaspoonful ground saffron

Remove the skin from the chicken. Using a sharp knife cut away as much of the flesh as possible from the carcass. Cut the chicken into convenient sized pieces.

In a pan heat the oil and fry the onion until it is golden brown. Add the ginger, garlic and pieces of chicken and fry rapidly for about 5 minutes. Add the spices, water and chicken stock cube and simmer for about half an hour. Blend the ground nuts with the yoghurt. Mix the saffron with a teaspoonful of hot water. Add the yoghurt and saffron and bring to the boil. Simmer for 10 minutes before serving.

Chicken Korma

(Serves 2–3)

2 green chillies
1 teaspoonful fresh ginger chopped
4 cloves garlic chopped
6 cardamoms
6 peppercorns
½ teaspoonful ground cinnamon
2 dessertspoonfuls dessicated coconut
2 dessertspoonfuls ground coriander
5 fl oz (142 ml) natural yoghurt
1 medium-sized onion chopped
4 chicken quarters each cut into two
1½ teaspoonfuls salt
1 tablespoonful lemon juice
½ chicken stock cube dissolved in 5 fl oz (142 ml) water
3 tablespoonfuls oil

Using a mortar and pestle grind together the first eight
ingredients. Heat the oil and fry the sliced onion until
brown. Remove the onions and in the same oil fry the
pieces of chicken until lightly browned. Add the onion
and the ground spices and stir for about 5 minutes. Add
the yoghurt and the stock and bring to the boil. Cover
and simmer for about 1 hour. Before serving add the
lemon juice and mix well.

Spicy Fried Chicken

(Serves 2–3)

½ teaspoonful chilli powder (optional)
1 teaspoonful garam masala
1 teaspoonful crushed garlic
1 teaspoonful crushed green ginger
salt to taste
6 drumsticks (chicken legs)
5 fl oz (142 ml) natural yoghurt
2 eggs
1 teaspoonful flour
1 teaspoonful crushed mint leaves
2 teaspoonfuls ground coriander
6 fl oz (170 ml) vegetable oil

Make a paste of the chilli powder, garam masala, garlic, ginger and salt and rub into the chicken. Pour yoghurt over the chicken and place in a large pan. Cook over a low heat and simmer for about 15 minutes until all the liquid has evaporated.

Make a batter of the egg yolks, flour, mint and coriander and rub over the pieces of chicken. Let the chicken so treated dry out in a shallow tray for a couple of hours.

Whisk egg whites. Heat oil in frying pan. Dip marinaded chicken in egg white and fry until golden brown.

This spicy fried chicken is delicious!

Chicken and Lentil Curry (Serves 3)

2 oz (56 gm) chana dhal
3 chicken quarters weighing about 2 lb (900 gm)
1 tablespoonful oil
1 medium-sized onion finely chopped
1 teaspoonful ground cumin
½ teaspoonful ground coriander
¼ teaspoonful ground cardamom
¼ teaspoonful ground cinnamon
1 teaspoonful salt
3 cloves garlic chopped
5 fl oz (142 ml) natural yoghurt
coriander leaves for garnish

Wash the dhal thoroughly. Soak overnight in 10 fl oz (284 ml) water. Put into a pan with another 5 fl oz (142 ml) water and boil for 5 minutes. Strain away the water. Wash and cut the chicken into convenient-sized pieces.

In a large pan heat the oil and fry the onion until it is golden brown. Increase the heat and fry the chicken until well browned. Add the spices and lastly the salt, garlic, yoghurt and lentils. Bring rapidly to the boil. Reduce the heat, cover and simmer for 45 minutes. Garnish with coriander leaves.

This is a mild chicken dish with the yoghurt adding an interesting sourness to the gravy.

Chicken with Dried Fruit

See under Kashmiri Lamb with Dried Fruit, page 57.

Tandouri Chicken

(Serves 2–3)

1 fresh chicken weighing approximately 3½ lb (1·5 kg)
1 medium-sized onion minced or finely chopped
3 cloves garlic chopped
1 teaspoonful fresh ginger chopped
10 fl oz (284 ml) natural yoghurt
rind and juice of 1 lemon
2 tablespoonfuls vinegar
1 teaspoonful paprika
2 teaspoonfuls garam masala
2 teaspoonfuls ground coriander
1 teaspoonful ground cumin
½ teaspoonful red food colouring

Remove the skin from the chicken and cut it into two. Using a sharp knife make slanting incisions 1 in. (2·5 cm) long in the chicken on each limb and breast, taking care not to cut through to the bone. In a non-metallic large bowl mix all the above ingredients. Marinade the chicken in this spicy yoghurt mixture for between 8 and 24 hours. Turn the chicken occasionally in the marinade to ensure that all sides become uniformly soaked.

Heat the oven to gas mark 6 (400° F). Place the chicken on a wire rack or a baking tray. Cover with foil and roast on the top shelf for 1 hour. Baste the chicken with the marinade mixture once during the cooking. Prior to serving, heat 2 tablespoonfuls of ghee and pour over the chicken halves and ignite.

Serve the chicken on a bed of lettuce garnished with onion rings, cucumber slices and lemon wedges. Serve with nan (see recipe on page 36).

The marinaded chicken pieces can also be grilled, barbecued or spit roasted.

Liver Curry

1 lb (454 gm) liver
5 fl oz (142 ml) water
1 fl oz (28 ml) vinegar
1 teaspoonful salt
¼ teaspoonful pepper
1 medium-sized onion finely sliced
2 cloves garlic chopped
½ teaspoonful chopped ginger
1 teaspoonful ground cumin
1 teaspoonful ground coriander
¼ teaspoonful garam masala
¼ teaspoonful ground turmeric
½ teaspoonful chilli powder
1 oz (28 gm) creamed coconut
2 fl oz (56 ml) vegetable oil

Cut the sliced liver into bite-sized pieces. Place in a pan with the water, vinegar, salt and pepper and boil for 10 minutes. Remove the pieces of liver and reserve the water in which the liver has been boiled. In another pan heat the oil and fry the pieces of liver for approximately 3 minutes on each side. Add the onion and the spices and continue to fry. Finally add the water and the creamed coconut and simmer for about 10 minutes. Serve with plain boiled rice.

Spicy Pork

(Serves 4–6)

1½ lb (680 gm) pork
8 oz (226 gm) lambs' liver
2 fl oz (56 ml) vegetable oil
2 large onions chopped
6 cloves garlic chopped
1 teaspoonful chopped ginger
¼ teaspoonful black pepper (freshly milled)
1 teaspoonful ground cumin
½ teaspoonful ground turmeric
2-in. (5-cm) stick cinnamon, ground
5 ground cloves
1 teaspoonful salt
1 fl oz (28 ml) vinegar

Cut the pork and the liver into bite-sized pieces and cook in 10 fl oz (284 ml) water for 30 minutes. In a large frying pan heat the oil and fry the pieces of pork and liver until brown. Transfer the meat to another receptacle. Fry the onions in the remaining fat and add the spices to it. Return the pork and liver to the pan and add the vinegar and 5 fl oz (142 ml) water. Simmer over a low heat until the meat is tender.

This is a popular way of cooking pork in Sri Lanka.

Pork Vindaloo

(Serves 4–5)

2 lb (1 kg) shoulder of pork
3 cloves garlic crushed
2 teaspoonfuls ginger finely chopped
2 teaspoonfuls ground coriander
1 teaspoonful ground cumin
1 teaspoonful chilli powder
12 peppercorns
1 teaspoonful ground cloves
1 teaspoonful ground cardamom
1 teaspoonful ground cinnamon
4 fl oz (113 ml) malt vinegar
1 teaspoonful salt
6 fl oz (170 ml) oil (preferably mustard oil)

Wash and cut the pork into 1-in. (2·5-cm) cubes. In a non-metallic bowl mix all the ingredients except the oil. Marinade the pork for 24 hours in the spicy vinegar. In a large heavy-bottomed pan heat the oil and toss in the meat and allow to brown lightly. Add the marinade and bring to the boil. Cover and simmer on a very low heat for 1½ hours.

This dish appears to have been invented by Portuguese settlers on the Indian subcontinent. It is now a speciality of their descendants in Goa.

Lamb in Yoghurt

(Serves 2–3)

1½ lb (680 gm) leg or shoulder of lamb
2 tablespoonfuls ghee or oil
½ teaspoonful ground coriander
¼ teaspoonful ground black pepper
¼ teaspoonful ground cloves
½ teaspoonful ground cardamom
¼ teaspoonful ground cinnamon
10 fl oz (284 ml) natural yoghurt
1 teaspoonful salt
2½ fl oz (71 ml) water
2 oz (56 gm) blanched almonds

Trim off the excess fat in the lamb and cut into pieces.
Heat the oil and fry the pieces of lamb until brown. Add
the spices and water and simmer until the liquid is
absorbed. (More water may be necessary for cooking the
shoulder of lamb.) Using a mortar and pestle pound the
almonds. Add the almonds and the yoghurt to the meat
and simmer for a further 10 minutes.

This is a mild curry, delicately flavoured, and is ideal as
an introduction to spicy food.

Spicy Lamb Curry

(Serves 4)

1½ lb (680 gm) lean lamb (leg or shoulder)
1 teaspoonful ground cumin
1 tablespoonful ground coriander
½ teaspoonful ground fennel
¼ teaspoonful ground cinnamon
½ teaspoonful ground cardamom
¼ teaspoonful ground cloves
¼ teaspoonful ground turmeric
1 teaspoonful chilli powder
2 tablespoonfuls ghee or oil
1 medium-sized onion finely chopped
1 teaspoonful fresh ginger chopped
2 cloves garlic
2 oz (56 gm) creamed coconut
10 fl oz (284 ml) hot water
1 teaspoonful salt

Cut the meat into 1-in. (2·5-cm) cubes. In a heavy-bottomed shallow pan lightly roast the spices over a low heat for approximately 6 minutes until they are a deep brown in colour. Heat the oil and fry the onions until they are golden brown. Add the meat, ginger and garlic and fry for a further 5 minutes. Add the spices and the rest of the ingredients and bring to the boil. Lower the heat and simmer for about 30 minutes or until the meat is tender. Serve with rice.

Kashmiri Lamb

(Serves 4)

1½ tablespoonfuls ghee or oil
1½ lb (680 gm) leg of lamb cubed
3 teaspoonfuls ground coriander
10 ground peppercorns
6 ground cloves
8 ground cardamoms
¼ teaspoonful ground cinnamon
1 teaspoonful ginger finely chopped
1 teaspoonful salt
5 fl oz (142 ml) water
1 oz (28 gm) ground almonds
3 fl oz (85 ml) double cream

Heat the oil until it is smoking hot. Add the cubes of
meat and allow to brown. Add the spices and salt and
the water and bring to the boil. Cover and simmer for 45
minutes. Just prior to serving mix the almonds and the
cream and add to the meat. Cook on a low heat until the
gravy starts to boil. Garnish with blanched almonds and
pistachio nuts.

Kashmiri Lamb with Dried Fruit

(Serves 4)

2 lb (1 kg) leg of lamb or mutton
1 teaspoonful allspice
½ teaspoonful ground black pepper
½ teaspoonful ground coriander
½ teaspoonful ground cumin
1½ teaspoonfuls salt
2 medium-sized onions finely sliced
2 teaspoonfuls finely chopped fresh ginger
2 cloves garlic finely chopped
10 fl oz (284 ml) natural yoghurt
2 oz (56 gm) ghee or butter
4 oz (113 gm) raisins
8 oz (226 gm) dried apricots
2 tablespoonfuls pistachio nuts

Trim off the fat and cut the meat into convenient-sized pieces. In a bowl mix the spices, the salt, the onions, ginger and garlic together with the yoghurt. Add the meat and allow to marinade for at least 6 hours.

Heat the ghee and fry the raisins, the apricots and the nuts for about 3 minutes, remove from the pan and set aside. Re-heat the ghee and add the meat and marinade and stir on a high flame for about 5 minutes. Cover and simmer for 1½ hours. Prior to serving add the dried fruit and nuts and cook for a further 5 minutes.

This Kashmiri delicacy can be adapted for cooking chicken with dried fruit in the same way as described here. Simply replace the lamb with de-boned chicken.

Kebabs (Serves 4)

1 lb (454 gm) minced meat
½ medium-sized onion ground or chopped finely
2 cloves garlic chopped
½ teaspoonful fresh ginger
1 teaspoonful ground coriander
15 mint leaves finely chopped
¼ teaspoonful ground cinnamon
¼ teaspoonful ground cloves
¼ teaspoonful ground cardamom
1 teaspoonful salt
½ teaspoonful tomato puree
¼ teaspoonful freshly milled black pepper

In a bowl mix all the ingredients thoroughly. Divide into 12 portions. Shape into flat discs and grill until browned on both sides.

Shikh Kebabs (1) (Serves 4)

1 lb (454 gm) minced meat
1 large onion finely chopped
3 cloves garlic finely chopped
1 teaspoonful finely chopped ginger
1 tablespoonful gram flour
1 tablespoonful chopped coriander leaves
1 teaspoonful chilli powder
¼ teaspoonful ground cinnamon
¼ teaspoonful ground cloves
¼ teaspoonful ground poppy seeds (optional)
½ teaspoonful freshly ground black pepper
a pinch of ground nutmeg
2 teaspoonfuls ground almonds

juice of half a lemon
1 egg
salt to taste
2 fl oz (56 ml) oil for grilling

Mix all the ingredients (except the oil) in a bowl and set aside to marinade for 45 minutes. Shape meat mixture into long sausage shapes and thread lengthwise onto 8 skewers. Place under grill turning skewers from time to time and brushing lightly with oil, until done. Before serving slide kebabs gently off the skewers and serve with crisp-fried onion rings.

Shikh Kebabs (2)   (Serves 4)

1 lb (454 gm) minced lean meat (lamb or beef)
1 large onion finely chopped
1 clove garlic finely chopped
1 green chilli finely chopped
1 tablespoonful finely chopped coriander leaves
1 teaspoonful garam masala
2 teaspoonfuls ground coriander seeds
½ teaspoonful ground cumin
1 teaspoonful chilli powder
½ teaspoonful ground turmeric
3 teaspoonfuls ground almonds
1 egg
salt to taste
2 fl oz (6 ml) oil for grilling

Mix all the ingredients (except the oil) in a bowl. Mould into long sausage shapes and thread lengthwise onto 8 greased skewers. Place under grill turning over and brushing occasionally with oil until done. Serve with crisp-fried onion rings.

Boti Kebabs   (Serves 4)

1½ lb (680 gm) leg of lamb, off the bone
3 teaspoonfuls ground coriander
½ teaspoonful ground turmeric
1 teaspoonful chilli powder
1 teaspoonful freshly ground black pepper
salt to taste
10 fl oz (284 ml) natural yoghurt
6 small onions

Cut the meat into 1-in. (2·5-cm) cubes. Mix the spices
and salt with the yoghurt in a large bowl. Mix in the
meat cubes and allow to marinade for at least 6 hours,
preferably overnight. Cut the onions into quarters and
separate layers. Thread cubes of meat and onion pieces
alternately on skewers, using 8 skewers in all. Cook
under grill, occasionally turning over, until done.

Mālu Cutlis (Fish Rissoles)   (Serves 4)

1 lb (454 gm) white fish (preferably cod)
3 green chillies finely chopped
¼ teaspoonful freshly milled black pepper
juice of 1 lemon
1 teaspoonful salt
1 large onion minced or finely chopped
1 teaspoonful ginger finely chopped
1 large potato boiled and mashed
2 eggs beaten
breadcrumbs
oil for deep frying

Remove the skin from the fish and wash thoroughly.
Place the fish in a pan and add sufficient water to cover

and bring to the boil. Cover and simmer until cooked (about 10 minutes depending on the type of fish). Flake the fish and in a bowl mix together with the spices, lemon juice, salt, onion, ginger and mashed potato. Divide into 12 portions and shape into flat discs. Dip into the beaten egg and roll in breadcrumbs. Heat the oil until it is smoking hot and fry a few rissoles at a time. Serve with rice.

This is a Sri Lankan speciality. Smaller-sized rissoles can be served with drinks.

Fish in Yoghurt Sauce (Serves 2)

1 lb (454 gm) filleted white fish, preferably cod
2 tablespoonfuls oil
1 medium-sized onion chopped
1 teaspoonful chopped ginger
3 cloves garlic chopped
½ teaspoonful salt
⅛ teaspoonful ground turmeric
½ teaspoonful ground cumin
1 teaspoonful ground coriander
½ teaspoonful garam masala
4 fl oz (113 ml) yoghurt
2 green chillies chopped

Wash the fish and cut each fillet into two. Heat the oil and fry the onion in it. Add the ginger, garlic, salt and spices. Add the yoghurt and the green chillies. Bring to the boil. Reduce the heat and slide in the pieces of fish. Simmer on a low heat for about 15 minutes. Serve with rice.

Fish Curry
(Serves 2)

1 lb (454 gm) haddock or cod fillets
juice of 1 lemon
1 oz (28 gm) creamed coconut
4 fl oz (113 ml) water
2 teaspoonfuls ground cumin powder
1 teaspoonful ground coriander
¼ teaspoonful ground turmeric
1 teaspoonful chilli powder
4 curry leaves if available
¼ teaspoonful ground cinnamon
½ teaspoonful salt
1 teaspoonful chopped ginger

Remove the skin from the fish. Cut each fillet into two. Add the lemon juice to the fish and allow to stand for 15 minutes. Wash thoroughly in cold water. In a shallow pan bring to the boil all the ingredients except the fish. Carefully slide in the pieces of fish and simmer on a low heat for 15 minutes. Do not stir but occasionally shake the pan. Serve with boiled rice and vegetables.

Mackerel in Tamarind
(Serves 2)

1 lb (454 gm) mackerel filleted
½ oz (14 gm) tamarind
½ teaspoonful ground cumin
¼ teaspoonful ground turmeric
¼ teaspoonful ground coriander
1 teaspoonful chilli powder
1 teaspoonful salt
1½ teaspoonfuls freshly finely chopped ginger
3 cloves garlic finely chopped

Wash the mackerel in cold water and cut each fillet into two. Soak the tamarind in 5 fl oz (142 ml) water for 15 minutes. Put the tamarind and the water into a pan and bring to the boil. Simmer for 5 minutes. Strain the tamarind and reserve the tamarind water. Place the fillets in a shallow pan. Mix the spices, ginger, garlic and the rest of the ingredients with the tamarind water. Pour over the fish and bring to the boil on a medium heat. Cover and simmer for 15 minutes. Serve with boiled rice, vegetables and pickle.

Prawn Curry   (Serves 2)

1 fl oz (28 ml) vegetable oil
½ medium-sized onion chopped
5 curry leaves if available
2 cloves garlic chopped
½ teaspoonful chopped ginger
1-in. (2·5-cm) piece cinnamon stick
½ teaspoonful ground turmeric
½ teaspoonful ground fenugreek
½ teaspoonful salt
½ teaspoonful chilli powder
juice of half a lemon
8 oz (226 gm) shelled prawns or shrimps
1 oz (28 gm) creamed coconut
4 fl oz (113 ml) water

Heat the oil and fry the onion until it is brown. Add the curry leaves, garlic and ginger and all the ingredients except the creamed coconut and the water. Fry for 5 minutes and then add the creamed coconut and the water. Bring to the boil, cover and simmer for 15 minutes. Serve with rice.

Prawn and Tomato Curry (Serves 2)

1 tablespoonful oil
1 small onion finely chopped
1 teaspoonful chopped ginger
3 cloves garlic chopped
1 teaspoonful vinegar
2 oz (56 gm) tomatoes fresh or canned
¼ teaspoonful ground turmeric
½ teaspoonful chilli powder (optional)
1 teaspoonful ground coriander
½ teaspoonful ground cumin
½ teaspoonful salt
8 oz (226 gm) shelled prawns or shrimps
5 fl oz (142 ml) water

Heat the oil and fry the onion until it is golden brown.
Add the ginger, garlic, vinegar, tomatoes, spices and
salt and the prawns, and fry for a further 3 minutes.
Add the water and bring to the boil. Cover and simmer
for about 15 minutes. Serve with rice or savoury rice
sticks (see recipe on p. 32).

Crab Curry

(Serves 3–4)

1 lb (454 gm) frozen or fresh crab meat
1 tablespoonful ghee or oil
1 medium-sized onion finely chopped
1 teaspoonful finely chopped ginger
2 cloves garlic chopped
a few curry leaves (optional)
juice of half a lime or lemon
1 tablespoonful ground coriander
½ tablespoonful ground cumin
¼ teaspoonful ground fennel
¼ teaspoonful ground turmeric
½ teaspoonful chilli powder
¼ teaspoonful ground cinnamon
1 teaspoonful salt
7½ fl oz (213 ml) of hot water
2 oz (56 gm) creamed coconut

Flake the crab meat. In a pan heat the oil and fry the onion in it. Add the ginger, garlic, curry leaves and the spices and salt and fry for a few minutes. Add the water and the creamed coconut, lime or lemon and bring to the boil. Lastly add the crab meat and simmer on a low flame for about 10 minutes. Serve with rice.

Vegetables and Lentils

Cauliflower Bhaji   (Serves 4)

2 tablespoonfuls oil
¼ tablespoonful mustard seed
2 medium-sized potatoes cut into matchsticks
1 medium-sized cauliflower cut into florets
3 cloves garlic
2 green chillies chopped
½ teaspoonful ground cumin
¼ teaspoonful ground coriander
¼ teaspoonful ground turmeric
¼ teaspoonful garam masala
1 teaspoonful salt

Heat oil in a pan. Add mustard seeds and allow to
sputter (the oil should not be burnt). Add the potatoes
and fry gently for about 3 minutes. Add the other
ingredients and stir fry for about 5 minutes. Pour
3½ fl oz (98 ml) warm water into the pan and allow to
simmer for about 15 minutes. To vary the flavour of this
dish a tablespoonful of desiccated coconut may be
added during cooking. Garnish with freshly chopped
coriander leaves when available.

Deep-fried Karella (Bitter Gourd)

(Serves 4)

1 lb (454 gm) karella
oil for deep frying
1 teaspoonful salt

Finely slice the karella and deep fry in the oil for about
10 minutes or until the slices are crisp. Sprinkle with salt
before serving.

Stuffed Cauliflower

(Serves 4)

2 tablespoonfuls coconut
4 oz (113 gm) cooked green peas
juice of half a lemon
1 teaspoonful ground cumin powder
½ teaspoonful chilli powder
1 green chilli
½ teaspoonful salt
1 medium-sized cauliflower
4 large lettuce leaves for garnishing
1 tablespoonful chopped coriander leaves for garnishing

Blend all the ingredients except the cauliflower, the
lettuce and the coriander leaves. Remove the outer
leaves from the cauliflower. Cut the main stem so that
the cauliflower remains stable when placed on a plate.
Cook the cauliflower gently in boiling water until just
tender, about 15 minutes. Remove from the pan and
place head downwards on a plate. Fill the crevices of the
cauliflower with the spicy coconut mixture, taking care
that the cauliflower does not disintegrate. Place the
cauliflower on a bed of lettuce. Sprinkle with chopped
coriander leaves. Serve at room temperature.

Dried Green Peas

1 medium-sized onion finely chopped
2 tablespoonfuls oil
1 teaspoonful ground coriander
½ teaspoonful ground cumin
½ teaspoonful fresh ginger finely chopped
1 green chilli chopped
¼ teaspoonful ground turmeric
¾ teaspoonful salt
8 oz (226 gm) dried green peas soaked overnight and
  boiled for 30 minutes
2 oz (56 gm) tamarind

Fry the onion and curry leaves in the oil. Add the spices and the drained green peas and set aside. In another pan add the tamarind to 5 fl oz (142 ml) water and let it simmer for 5 minutes. Mash the tamarind with a fork and then strain it. Add the strained tamarind to the peas and allow to cook for a further 5 minutes.

Cabbage and Split Peas (Serves 4)

2 tablespoonfuls oil
¼ teaspoonful mustard seed
a few curry leaves
2 red chillies
8 oz (226 gm) split peas soaked for 4 hours and drained
a pinch of asafoetida
¼ teaspoonful ground turmeric powder
1 teaspoonful cumin seed
1 teaspoonful salt
1 lb (454 gm) cabbage cut into ½-in. (1–2-cm) slices and
  coarsely chopped

Heat oil. Add mustard seeds and allow to sputter (the oil should not be burnt). Add the curry leaves and dry chillies and the split peas. Stir fry for 5 minutes. Add the other spices and the cabbage and stir fry over a low heat until the cabbage is cooked. (Use a heavy-bottomed skillet for cooking.)

Cabbage with Coconut (Serves 4)

8 oz (226 gm) spring greens or cabbage leaves finely
  shredded as for coleslaw
½ medium-sized onion chopped
2 cloves garlic
¼ teaspoonful ground cumin
½ teaspoonful ground coriander
¼ teaspoonful ground turmeric
1 teaspoonful salt
2 tablespoonfuls unsweetened desiccated coconut
2 green chillies finely chopped
1 tablespoonful water

In a bowl mix all the ingredients thoroughly. Using a heavy-bottomed frying pan stir fry the cabbage on a low flame for about 5 minutes.

Leeks and White Cabbage (Serves 3–4)

8 oz (226 gm) white cabbage
8 oz (226 gm) leeks
1 tablespoonful oil
¼ teaspoonful mustard seed
½ teaspoonful cumin seed
¼ teaspoonful ground turmeric
½ teaspoonful salt
4 curry leaves when available
2 or 3 whole red chillies (optional)
a pinch of asafoetida (optional)

Wash and finely shred the cabbage and the leeks. In a large frying pan heat the oil and allow the mustard seeds to sputter in it. (The lid should be left on.) Add the spices and the vegetables and stir. Fry on a low heat for about 7 minutes.

Leeks in Gram Flour   (Serves 3)

1 tablespoonful oil
¼ teaspoonful mustard seed
¼ teaspoonful ground turmeric
¼ teaspoonful chilli powder
½ teaspoonful salt
1 lb (454 gm) leeks cut into 1-in. (2·5-cm) pieces
7½ fl oz (213 ml) water
1 oz (28 gm) gram flour

Heat the oil, add the mustard seed and allow to sputter.
Add the rest of the spices and lastly the leeks. Toss the
leeks for a few seconds in the pan. Add the water, bring
to the boil and allow the leeks to cook over a low heat
(about 5 minutes).

   In a bowl mix 2 tablespoonfuls of gram flour with
sufficient water to make a stiff paste. Take the pan off
the heat, and work the gram flour paste into the leeks.
When mixed thoroughly return to a low heat and allow
to cook for 5 minutes.

Potato Curry   (Serves 4)

1½ lb (680 gm) potatoes
1 tablespoonful oil
1 medium-sized onion finely chopped
3 cloves garlic chopped
5 curry leaves if available
2 green chillies chopped
1 teaspoonful ground cumin
1 teaspoonful ground coriander
1½ teaspoonfuls salt
¼ teaspoonful ground turmeric
1 oz (28 gm) creamed coconut
½ teaspoonful ground roasted mustard seed

Peel and wash the potatoes and cut into 1-in. (2·5-cm) cubes. Heat the oil and fry the onion until it is golden brown. Add the garlic and the curry leaves, also the rest of the ingredients except the mustard powder. Add 15 fl oz (426 ml) water and bring to the boil. Cover and simmer for 10 minutes, or until the potatoes are cooked. Prior to serving sprinkle with the mustard powder.

To make ground roasted mustard seed, put the mustard seeds in a heavy-bottomed pan and over a low heat roast the mustard seeds for about 5 minutes, stirring all the time. Cool and grind and then store in an airtight container.

Potato and Pea Curry (Serves 4)

2 large onions
3 cloves garlic
2 green chillies
1-in. (2·5-cm) piece of ginger
2½ fl oz (71 ml) ghee or vegetable oil
4 medium tomatoes
½ teaspoonful ground turmeric
1 teaspoonful ground coriander
1 teaspoonful garam masala
½ teaspoonful red chilli powder
3 medium-sized potatoes
1 lb (454 gm) green peas
½ tablespoonful salt
coriander leaves for garnish

Grind onions, garlic, green chillies and ginger. Melt ghee and fry mixture until brown. Add tomatoes, turmeric, coriander, garam masala, red chilli powder, potatoes and peas, stirring slowly. Then add 20 fl oz

(568 ml) water and the salt. Bring to the boil and simmer until potatoes are cooked. Garnish with coriander leaves before serving.

Spiced Green Beans (Serves 3)

1 tablespoonful oil
¼ teaspoonful mustard seed
½ medium-sized onion finely chopped
¼ teaspoonful ground turmeric
½ teaspoonful ground cumin
¼ teaspoonful ground coriander
½ teaspoonful salt
12 oz (340 gm) beans cut into pieces
3 fl oz (85 ml) water

Heat the oil in a frying pan and over a low flame sputter the mustard seeds in it. Add the onion and stir fry for about 3 minutes. Add the spices and the salt and the beans, lastly the water. Bring rapidly to the boil. Simmer on a low heat for 10 minutes.

Black-eyed Beans (Serves 4–6)

8 oz (226 gm) black-eyed beans
½ medium-sized onion finely chopped
1 tablespoonful cooking oil
¼ teaspoonful ground turmeric
1 teaspoonful ground cumin
½ teaspoonful ground coriander
½ teaspoonful garam masala
1 teaspoonful salt

Wash and soak the beans in cold water for 2 hours. Put the beans in a pan with 7½ fl oz (213 ml) water and bring to the boil. Lower the heat and simmer until all the water is absorbed.

In another pan heat the oil and fry the onion until it is golden brown. Add the spices, salt and lastly the beans and stir over a low heat for about a minute. Garnish with coriander leaves and serve with chappatis or rice.

Tomato Curry   (Serves 3)

1 tablespoonful oil
½ medium-sized onion finely chopped
¼ teaspoonful ground fenugreek
1½ teaspoonfuls ground coriander
a few curry leaves (optional)
1 teaspoonful ground cumin
¼ teaspoonful ground turmeric
1 teaspoonful salt
2 oz (56 gm) creamed coconut
1 lb (454 gm) firm ripe tomatoes chopped
2 green chillies chopped

Heat oil and fry onion in it. Add spices, salt and the rest of the ingredients and simmer until tender (about 20 minutes). For an interesting variation cut boiled eggs in half and add to the curry before serving.

Courgettes (Baby Marrow or Zucchini)
(Serves 4)

1 lb (454 gm) courgettes
2 fl oz (56 ml) vegetable oil
¼ teaspoonful mustard seed
1 medium-sized onion chopped
5 curry leaves if available
4 cloves garlic chopped
a pinch of ground turmeric
½ teaspoonful salt
a pinch of asafoetida
1 teaspoonful ground cumin
2 green chillies chopped
3 tablespoonfuls water

Wash and cut the courgettes into ¼-in. (½-cm) pieces. Heat the oil and sputter the mustard seeds in it. (The lid should be kept on while sputtering.) Fry the onion, curry leaves and garlic for about 3 minutes. Add the spices and the rest of the ingredients. Cook on a low to medium heat for about 15 minutes.

Spicy Marrow
(Serves 6)

3 lb (1·3 kg) marrow
1 tablespoonful oil
¼ teaspoonful mustard seed
1 medium-sized onion finely sliced
1 teaspoonful chopped ginger
5 curry leaves (if available)
½ teaspoonful ground turmeric
1½ teaspoonfuls salt
1 teaspoonful ground cumin
1½ teaspoonfuls ground coriander

¼ teaspoonful chilli powder
2 green chillies chopped (optional)
2 tomatoes chopped
1 tablespoonful chopped coriander leaves for garnishing

Wash the marrow and cut it lengthwise and discard the seeds. Cut into 1½-in. (4-cm) cubes. Heat the oil and on a low flame sputter the mustard seeds in it. (The lid should be kept on.) Add the onions, ginger and curry leaves and fry for about 5 minutes. Add spices and the rest of the ingredients. Lastly add the marrow. Cook uncovered on a very low heat stirring occasionally to prevent the marrow from sticking to the bottom of the pan. Garnish with coriander leaves.

Mushroom Curry   (Serves 4)

1 lb (454 gm) mushrooms
4 fl oz (113 ml) vegetable oil
2 medium-sized onions chopped
½ teaspoonful ground turmeric
1 teaspoonful salt
4 cloves garlic chopped
1 teaspoonful ground cumin
½ teaspoonful chilli powder
juice of half a lemon

Clean mushrooms and cut into quarters. Heat oil and fry onions in it until brown. Mix in the mushrooms, turmeric, salt, garlic, cumin and chilli. Reduce heat and stir continuously until mushrooms are cooked. Add the lemon before serving.

Spinach, Stir-fried (Serves 2)

1 tablespoonful oil
1 onion chopped
1 teaspoonful ground cumin
½ teaspoonful ground coriander
½ teaspoonful salt
1 lb (454 gm) spinach chopped
2 ripe tomatoes chopped

Heat oil and gently fry the onion in it. Add the spices
and the chopped spinach a little at a time and continue
to stir. Finally add the tomatoes and cook uncovered for
3 minutes. Spring cabbage or broccoli can be substituted
for the spinach with the omission of the tomatoes.

White Radish with Coconut (Serves 3–4)

2 tablespoonfuls oil
¼ teaspoonful mustard seed
1 medium-sized onion chopped
¼ teaspoonful ground turmeric
1 oz (28 gm) desiccated coconut
a pinch of asafoetida
1 green chilli chopped
1 teaspoonful salt
1 lb (454 gm) white radish cut into ¼-in. (½-cm) thick
   strips

Heat the oil. Add the mustard seeds and allow them to
sputter. Add the onion, the spices, the radish and
5 fl oz (142 ml) water and simmer until cooked (about
7 minutes).

Aubergines

(Serves 4)

2 oz (56 gm) creamed coconut
4 fl oz (113 ml) water
2 green chillies chopped
a few curry leaves
1 medium-sized onion finely chopped
1½ fl oz (42 ml) vinegar
1 teaspoonful sugar
½ teaspoonful ground roasted mustard seed
1½ teaspoonfuls ground coriander
1½ teaspoonfuls ground cumin
1-in. (2·5-cm) piece of cinnamon
¼ teaspoonful ground turmeric
1 teaspoonful salt
1 lb (454 gm) aubergines cut into ½-in. (1-cm) cubes and
   deep-fried until golden brown

Allow the creamed coconut to dissolve in the water over a low heat. Add all the ingredients except the aubergines to the dissolved creamed coconut and cook for 7 minutes. Once this sauce is thick add the aubergines and simmer for a further 5 minutes.

Fried Aubergines

(Serves 4)

3 oz (85 gm) gram flour
1½ teaspoonfuls salt
¼ teaspoonful chilli powder
1 lb (454 gm) aubergines sliced to ⅛-in. (3-mm) thickness
oil for frying

Mix the flour, salt and chilli powder. Dust the pieces of aubergine on both sides in the seasoned flour and shallow fry for about 3 minutes on each side.

Curried Fried Bhindi (Okra or Lady's Fingers) (Serves 4)

1 lb (454 gm) bhindi
oil for deep frying
1 tablespoonful oil
1 small onion finely chopped
½ teaspoonful chilli powder (optional)
¼ teaspoonful ground turmeric
½ teaspoonful ground cumin
¼ teaspoonful ground coriander
¾ teaspoonful salt
10 fl oz (284 ml) water
1 oz (28 gm) creamed coconut

Wash and dry the bhindi. Trim the tops and tails and cut into 1-in. (2·5 cm) pieces. Deep fry the pieces until they are golden brown. In a pan heat a tablespoonful of oil and fry the onion until it is lightly browned. Add the spices, the water and the creamed coconut and bring to the boil. Just prior to serving add the bhindi and rapidly bring to the boil. Serve with rice.

Stuffed Bhindi (Okra or Lady's Fingers) (Serves 3)

3 oz (85 gm) desiccated coconut
1 teaspoonful salt
½ teaspoonful ground cumin
¼ teaspoonful chilli powder
¼ teaspoonful ground turmeric
juice of half a lemon
1 lb (454 gm) bhindi

In a bowl mix all the ingredients except the bhindi. Slit each bhindi lengthwise and carefully force in a small quantity of the coconut filling. In a large frying pan heat 3 fl oz (85 ml) oil. Carefully arrange the bhindis in the frying pan and allow to cook for 5 minutes. Turn each bhindi over and cook for a further 5 minutes adding more cooking oil if necessary.

Avial (Mixed Vegetables in Yoghurt Sauce) (Serves 4)

1 tablespoonful oil
½ teaspoonful ground turmeric
1 teaspoonful ground coriander
3 green chillies finely chopped
3 cups of mixed vegetables cut into bite-sized pieces (e.g. cauliflower, carrots, courgettes, aubergines, beans, sweet potato etc)
1½ teaspoonfuls salt
15 fl oz (426 ml) water
8 oz (226 gm) desiccated coconut
10 fl oz (284 ml) natural yoghurt

In a medium-sized saucepan heat the oil. Add the spices and vegetables and lightly toss the vegetables. Add salt and water and bring to the boil. Lower the heat and simmer for 10 minutes. Add the coconut and the yoghurt and bring to the boil. Allow to boil for 3 minutes before removing from the heat. Serve with rice.

This is a Kerala (South Indian) speciality and served with rice makes an excellent vegetarian meal.

Curried Stuffed Peppers (Serves 3)

1 lb (454 gm) green peppers (preferably small peppers, about
   6 in number)
2 tablespoonfuls oil
6 oz (170 gm) onions chopped finely
1 teaspoonful ground cumin
1 teaspoonful ground coriander
¾ teaspoonful salt
½ teaspoonful ground turmeric
½ teaspoonful chilli powder
7 oz (198 gm) potatoes boiled and cubed

In a large pan bring 50 fl oz (1·42 l) water to the boil.
Add the peppers and blanch for 5 minutes. Remove
from the water, cut round the stem and remove the
seeds. In a small frying pan heat the oil and soften the
onions in it. Add the spices and the potatoes and mix
thoroughly. Remove from heat and allow the filling to
cool. Divide into 6 portions and fill each pepper with
this spicy filling.

For the curry you need:

½ medium-sized onion finely chopped
6 cloves
6 cardamoms
2 cloves garlic finely chopped
2 teaspoonfuls ginger finely chopped
1 teaspoonful salt
a few pieces of cinnamon stick
¼ teaspoonful ground turmeric
½ teaspoonful chilli powder
1 teaspoonful ground coriander
1 teaspoonful ground cumin
1½ oz (42 gm) creamed coconut
30 fl oz (852 ml) water

In a medium-sized pan bring all the above ingredients to the boil. Lower the heat and simmer for 20 minutes. Add the stuffed peppers and cook on a low heat for a further 10 minutes. The gravy should be similar to a thick coating sauce. Serve with rice.

Instead of a potato filling the peppers can be stuffed with minced meat or flaked white fish.

This is a popular Sri Lankan accompaniment to a curry meal.

Cashew-nut Curry   (Serves 3–4)

8 oz (226 gm) cashew-nuts
1 tablespoonful oil
1 medium-sized onion finely chopped
1½ teaspoonfuls ground coriander
1 teaspoonful ground cumin
¼ teaspoonful ground turmeric
2 cloves
2 cardamoms
2 pieces of cinnamon stick
1 teaspoonful salt
1 oz (28 gm) creamed coconut

Add ½ a teaspoonful of bicarbonate of soda to 30 fl oz (852 ml) cold water. Soak the cashew-nuts in it for 8 hours. Drain away the water and wash the cashew-nuts. In a pan heat the oil and fry the onion until lightly browned. Add the spices, salt and cashew-nuts and mix thoroughly. Add the creamed coconut and 5 fl oz (142 ml) water and bring to the boil. Lower the heat and simmer for 15 minutes.

This is a Sri Lankan favourite and could be used as a main source of protein for a vegetarian meal.

Pumpkin Curry

(Serves 3–4)

1 lb (454 gm) pumpkin
2 cloves garlic crushed
½ medium-sized onion finely chopped
2 tablespoonfuls desiccated coconut
1 teaspoonful oil
¼ teaspoonful mustard seed
a few curry leaves when available
1 teaspoonful ground coriander
½ teaspoonful ground cumin
¼ teaspoonful turmeric
1 teaspoonful salt
1 oz (28 gm) creamed coconut
5 fl oz (142 ml) hot water

Peel off the skin and remove the seeds from the pumpkin. Cut into 2-in. (5-cm) cubes. In a heavy-bottomed frying pan (over a low heat) roast the coconut until lightly browned. Grind the garlic, onion and the coconut to a smooth paste.

In a pan heat the oil, add the mustard seeds and cook covered on a low heat until the seeds sputter. Add the curry leaves, spices and salt. Add the coconut paste and the pumpkin. Lastly add the creamed coconut and the water and bring rapidly to the boil. Cover and simmer for 10–15 minutes. Serve with rice.

Spiced Fried Potatoes (Serves 4)

1 lb (454 gm) potatoes
oil for deep frying
8 oz (226 gm) finely sliced onions
1 tablespoonful vegetable oil
1 tablespoonful maldive fish, powdered (when available)
a few curry leaves
½ teaspoonful salt
½ teaspoonful chilli powder
1 dessertspoonful lime or lemon juice

Wash the potatoes and place in a saucepan. Cover with cold water and bring rapidly to the boil. Allow to boil for 5 minutes. Drain away the water and peel the potatoes. Cut the potatoes into ¾-in. (2-cm) cubes. Heat the oil and deep fry the potatoes until lightly browned. Deep fry the onions until golden brown.

In a frying pan or skillet heat the tablespoonful of oil. Fry the maldive fish for about 30 seconds. Add the curry leaves, the salt and chilli powder and mix well. Lastly toss in the potatoes and the onions and stir. Remove from heat. Prior to serving add the lemon or lime juice.

This is a Sri Lankan speciality and is usually eaten with fried rice or any special rice dish.

Lentils (1)   (Serves 6)

12 oz (339 gm) Masur lentils (the orange lentil)
1 medium-sized onion finely shred
2 tablespoonfuls oil
¼ teaspoonful mustard seed
2 green chillies chopped
a few curry leaves (optional)
1 teaspoonful ground cumin
1 teaspoonful ground coriander
¼ teaspoonful turmeric powder
¼ teaspoonful ground fenugreek
2 teaspoonfuls salt

Wash the lentils under running water in a sieve. Put in a pan with 30 fl oz (852 ml) water and half the onion and boil slowly until the lentils are cooked and quite mushy.

In another pan heat the oil and sputter the mustard seeds in it. Fry the remainder of the onion until golden brown. Add the rest of the spices and lastly the lentils. Allow to simmer for 15 minutes.

To vary the flavour a small can of tomatoes can be added before the final simmering.

Lentils (2)

(Serves 4–6)

8 oz (226 gm) Masur lentils (the orange lentil)
25 fl oz (710 ml) cups water
3 tablespoonfuls oil
¼ teaspoonful mustard seed
1 medium-sized onion finely sliced
4 dried red chillies
2-in (5-cm) stick cinnamon
1 teaspoonful maldive fish (optional)
¼ teaspoonful ground turmeric
⅛ teaspoonful ground fenugreek
½ teaspoonful ground cumin
½ teaspoonful ground coriander
1½ teaspoonfuls salt
1 oz (28 gm) creamed coconut
juice of half a lime or lemon

Wash the lentils in a sieve under running cold water.
Put the water and the lentils in a pan and bring to the
boil. Lower the heat and cook uncovered for about 20
minutes, stirring occasionally.

Heat the oil and add the mustard seeds. Put the lid on
and allow the seeds to sputter. Add the onion and fry
until golden brown. Add the red chillies, the spices and
the salt. Add the cooked lentils and lastly the grated
creamed coconut. Simmer for 10 minutes. Before serving
add the lemon juice. Serve with plain boiled rice.

Chick Peas (Serves 6)

8 oz (226 gm) chick peas
2 tablespoonfuls cooking oil
1 medium-sized onion finely sliced
2 green chillies chopped (optional)
1 teaspoonful ground coriander
1 teaspoonful ground cumin
½ teaspoonful chopped ginger
¼ teaspoonful ground cinnamon
¼ teaspoonful ground cloves
3 cardamoms crushed
1 teaspoonful salt
1 tablespoonful lemon juice
1 tablespoonful coriander leaves for garnishing

Wash and soak the chick peas in 30 fl oz (852 ml) of water for at least 8 hours. Put the chick peas and 10 fl oz (284 ml) water in a pan and bring to the boil. Simmer for 30 minutes.

In another pan heat the oil and fry the onion in it. Add the spices and the salt and cooked chick peas and any remaining liquid in which the peas were boiled. Add the lemon juice and mix thoroughly. Garnish with the coriander leaves just before serving.

Chana Dhal

8 oz (226 gm) Chana dhal
2 tablespoonfuls oil
½ medium-sized onion finely sliced
1 teaspoonful chopped ginger
3 green chillies chopped
½ teaspoonful ground cumin
1 teaspoonful garam masala
1 teaspoonful salt
¼ teaspoonful ground turmeric
1 teaspoonful tomato puree

Wash and soak the dhal for about 6 hours. Put 15 fl oz (426 ml) of water and the dhal in a pan and boil until the water has evaporated.

Heat the oil and fry the onion until golden brown. Add the ginger and the spices and tomato puree. Lastly toss in the dhal and boil on a low flame for about 5 minutes.

Lentil Rissoles (Vadé)

(Serves 6)

8 oz (226 gm) Masur dhal (the orange lentil)
1½ teaspoonfuls powdered dry fish (optional)
¼ teaspoonful ground turmeric
½ teaspoonful chilli powder
1 teaspoonful salt
1 medium-sized onion finely chopped
10 curry leaves (or bay leaves) broken in small pieces
3 green chillies finely chopped
vegetable oil for deep frying

Wash dhal in cold water several times. Place washed dhal in a bowl with 10 fl oz (284 ml) cold water and allow to soak for 3 hours. Grind dhal in a blender. Mix in all the other ingredients. Drop dessertspoonfuls of the thick lentil batter into the hot fat. Turn and brown on both sides. Drain on kitchen paper and serve hot. Yields about 25. This provides a nourishing tea-time savoury.

This is a popular snack in South India and Sri Lanka.

Moong Dhal with Spinach (Serves 6)

12 oz (339 gm) yellow moong dhal
2 tablespoonfuls oil
¼ teaspoonful mustard seed
5 curry leaves if available
1 teaspoonful chopped ginger
¼ teaspoonful ground turmeric
1 teaspoonful ground cumin
1½ teaspoonfuls salt
2 tablespoonfuls spring onions chopped
4 green chillies chopped
4 oz (113 gm) chopped spinach

Wash the lentils and bring to the boil with 30 fl oz (852 ml) water. Cover and simmer for about 30 minutes.
    In another pan heat the oil, add the mustard seeds and allow to sputter. Add the curry leaves and the ginger and the spices. Fry for a few minutes. Add the salt and the spring onions and green chillies and pour in the boiled lentils. Bring to the boil and cook for 5 minutes. Lastly add the chopped spinach and allow to simmer for about 5 minutes. Serve with rice or chappatis.

Thur Dhal

12 oz (339 gm) Thur lentils
1 tablespoonful oil
¼ teaspoonful mustard seed
3 cloves garlic chopped
a pinch of asafoetida (optional)
¼ teaspoonful ground turmeric
1 teaspoonful salt
½ oz (14 gm) tamarind dissolved in 2 fl oz (56 ml) boiling
   water
2 green chillies chopped
6 fl oz (170 ml) water

Wash and soak the lentils overnight in 30 fl oz (852 ml) water. Cook the lentils in the same amount of water for 35 minutes.

In another pan heat the oil and sputter the mustard seeds in it. Add the garlic and fry for 3 minutes. Add the spices, salt and the strained tamarind water. Finally add the lentils and the green chillies and water and bring to the boil. Simmer for 5 minutes. Serve with plain boiled rice.

Dosa (Lentil Pancakes)   (Serves 6)

8 oz (226 gm) split urad dhal (the white lentil)
1 lb (454 gm) rice
3 teaspoonfuls salt

Wash the lentils in a sieve until the water runs clear.
Soak overnight in 20 fl oz (568 ml) water. Wash the rice
thoroughly and also soak overnight in 30 fl oz (852 ml)
water. Drain the water away from the lentils and the rice.
Grind the lentils to a smooth paste with 2½ fl oz (71 ml)
water. Grind the rice separately in 5 fl oz (142 ml) water.
Mix the ground lentils and the rice and salt in a bowl
and leave in a warm place for 36 hours. The mixture
should be fermented and frothy.

Heat a griddle or a heavy-bottomed frying pan.
Lightly grease the surface with a teaspoonful of oil. Pour
2 tablespoonfuls of the dosa mixture and using the back
of a metal spoon spread evenly over the surface of the
pan. Pour ½ teaspoonful of oil round the circumference
of the dosa. Using a spatula turn over and allow to
brown lightly.

Repeat the cooking process until all the batter is used.
Serve with coconut chutney. Makes about 25.

This is a South Indian speciality, also common to Sri
Lanka.

Salads and Chutneys

Onion Salad (Serves 4)

8 oz (226 gm) onions
juice of a lemon
½ teaspoonful salt
2 green chillies finely chopped
¼ teaspoonful freshly milled black pepper

Using a cucumber slicer finely slice the onions. If a slicer is not available finely slice the onions by hand. Mix all the ingredients and leave for at least 1 hour before serving. Before serving finely sliced tomatoes can be added.

Lettuce with Peanut Dressing (Serves 4)

2 fl oz (56 ml) oil
¼ teaspoonful mustard seed
¼ teaspoonful cumin seed
a pinch of ground turmeric
½ teaspoonful salt
1 fl oz (28 ml) lemon juice
1 lettuce washed and dried
½ cucumber sliced
2 oz (56 gm) peanuts coarsely ground

Heat oil and sputter the mustard seeds in it. Add the cumin seed, turmeric and salt. Remove from heat and add lemon juice. Allow the dressing to get cold before tossing into the other salad ingredients.

Cucumber Raita (Serves 6)

10 fl oz (284 ml) natural yoghurt
½ teaspoonful salt
¼ teaspoonful sugar
¼ teaspoonful ground black pepper
½ lb (226 gm) cucumber finely sliced
1 tablespoonful chopped coriander leaves

In a bowl mix the yoghurt, salt, sugar and pepper. Add the cucumber and garnish with coriander leaves.

Carrot Sambol (Serves 4)

4 oz (113 gm) carrot finely grated
¾ teaspoonful salt
¼ teaspoonful freshly milled black pepper
1 tablespoonful lemon juice
1 oz (28 gm) desiccated coconut
coriander leaves for garnish

Mix all the ingredients in a bowl. Garnish with a tablespoonful of chopped coriander leaves.

Mint Sambol (Serves 4)

2 oz (56 gm) mint leaves
7 peppercorns
½ oz (14 gm) onions
¼ teaspoonful sugar
3 cloves
2 green chillies
½ teaspoonful salt
juice of half a lime or lemon

Grind the ingredients to a smooth paste.

An excellent sambol for accompanying lamb dishes.

Dried Prawn Sambol (Serves 6)

2 oz (56 gm) dried prawns
10 fl oz (284 ml) oil
8 oz (226 gm) onions finely sliced
3 cloves garlic chopped
½ teaspoonful chopped ginger
½ teaspoonful salt
½ teaspoonful chilli powder
1 dessertspoonful lemon juice

Wash the prawns and place in an ovenproof dish and roast at gas mark ½ (280° F) for 1 hour. Grind the prawns in an electric blender. Heat the oil and fry the finely sliced onion until golden brown. Drain the onions on kitchen paper.

In another pan heat one tablespoonful of oil and fry the garlic and ginger for 3 minutes. Add the dried prawn powder and continue to fry on a low heat for about 5 minutes. Add the salt and the chilli powder and lastly

the onions, and mix thoroughly. Remove from heat and
add the lemon juice.

Ideal accompaniment to rice dishes, particularly to pilafs.

Date Chutney (Serves 6–8 generous helpings)

6 fl oz (170 ml) malt vinegar
3 tablespoonfuls brown sugar
4 oz (113 gm) chopped dates
2 cloves garlic finely chopped
½ teaspoonful ginger finely chopped
½ teaspoonful salt
1 teaspoonful paprika
1 oz (28 gm) sultanas

Put the vinegar and the sugar in a pan and bring rapidly
to the boil. Reduce the heat and add the dates, garlic
and the ginger. Cook on a low heat for 15 minutes
stirring all the time. Add the salt, paprika and the
sultanas and cook for a further 5 minutes.

This sweet and sour chutney is an ideal accompaniment
to any rice meal, particularly to pilafs and biriani.

Tomato Chutney

3½ lb (1·5 kg) firm ripe tomatoes
2 lb (900 gm) onions finely chopped
2 lb (900 gm) sugar
3½ oz (70 gm) brown sugar
½ oz (14 gm) ginger, finely chopped
1½ teaspoonfuls salt
¼ oz (7 gm) chilli powder
20 fl oz (568 ml) malt vinegar

Put the tomatoes into a pan of boiling water for 3 minutes. Remove the tomatoes and cool them by immersing in a bowl of cold water. Peel off the skins. Chop the tomatoes and place all the ingredients (except the vinegar) in a pan. Cook for about 1 hour on a low heat to a thick consistency. Add the vinegar and cook for another 10 minutes. Pour the chutney while hot into dry sterile jars. Seal and store in a cool dry place.

Coconut Chutney (1)   (Serves 4)

½ fl oz (14 ml) oil
½ tablespoonful split peas
1 oz (28 gm) tamarind
2 tablespoonfuls coconut
2 green chillies
½ teaspoonful salt

Heat the oil and fry the split peas in it. Soak the tamarind in 5 fl oz (142 ml) boiling water. Mash with a fork, strain through a sieve and reserve the liquid. Put all the ingredients, including the strained tamarind liquid, into a liquidizer and blend for 5 minutes.

Coconut Chutney (2)   (Serves 4)

4 oz (113 gm) coconut – if desiccated is used soak in
  ½ fl oz (14 ml) of milk
2 teaspoonfuls chilli powder
juice of half a lemon
1 teaspoonful salt
1 oz (28 gm) onions finely grated
¼ teaspoonful freshly ground black pepper
1 clove garlic crushed

Mix all the ingredients in a bowl. If a mortar and pestle is available pound all the ingredients a little at a time. Serve at room temperature. A small bunch of finely chopped spring onions added to this recipe makes for an interesting variation.

This is a popular Sri Lankan side dish and is eaten with rice and curry meals.

Seeni Sambol   (Serves 6)

oil for deep frying
1½ lb (680 gm) onions finely sliced
½ oz (14 gm) tamarind
1 tablespoonful oil
1½ teaspoonfuls maldive fish or dried prawns (optional)
4 cloves garlic finely chopped
1½ teaspoonfuls ginger finely chopped
1 oz (28 gm) creamed coconut, dissolved in 5 fl oz (142 ml)
  boiling water
1½ teaspoonfuls salt
1 tablespoonful chilli powder
1 teaspoonful sugar

4 pods of cardamoms
2 pieces cinnamon stick

Heat the oil and deep fry the onions, a little at a time until golden brown. Drain on absorbent paper.

Soak the tamarind in 5 fl oz (142 ml) water for about 20 minutes. Put the tamarind and the water into a pan and cook on a low heat for about 5 minutes. Strain the tamarind liquid and set aside.

In a small pan heat the tablespoonful of oil and add the maldive fish or prawns to it. Allow to fry for about 5 minutes. Add the garlic and the ginger, and then the rest of the ingredients including the tamarind water. Bring to the boil and simmer on a very low heat until the liquid has evaporated.

This is a Sri Lankan speciality and is relished as an accompaniment to any rice and curry meal. It is eaten in small quantities, and loosely translated means 'sugar sambol' despite the many other ingredients that go to make it.

Lemon Pickle   (Serves 10)

1 lb (454 gm) fresh lemons
¼ teaspoonful ground turmeric
2 tablespoonfuls salt
½ teaspoonful ground fenugreek
1 teaspoonful mustard seed
1 tablespoonful chilli powder
2 tablespoonfuls oil

Wash the lemons. Place them in a pan with 20 fl oz (568 ml) water and the tumeric and bring to the boil. Allow the lemons to continue boiling for 7 minutes. Drain away the water.

On a plate cut each lemon into 8 sections. Remove the pips. Sprinkle with salt and store in a dry jam jar for 1 week, remembering to turn the lemons over every day.

In a heavy-bottomed frying pan over a low heat lightly brown the fenugreek and the mustard seed, taking care not to let it burn. Cool and then grind. Mix the mustard, fenugreek and the chilli into the lemons. Pour the oil on top of the lemons to act as an air barrier. Store in a cool place.

Mixed Pickle (Serves 10)

¼ teaspoonful ground turmeric
1 teaspoonful salt
60 fl oz (1·7 l) boiling water
8 oz (226 gm) pickling onions
8 oz (226 gm) carrots
2 oz (56 gm) green chillies
4 oz (113 gm) french beans cut into matchsticks
1 tablespoonful mustard freshly ground
1 teaspoonful chilli powder
1½ teaspoonfuls sugar
1 teaspoonful salt
1 teaspoonful fresh ginger ground
3 cloves garlic crushed
4 fl oz (113 ml) malt vinegar

In a pan add the turmeric and salt to the boiling water. Blanch the onions and the carrots for 5 minutes. Blanch the green chillies and the beans for 2 minutes. Drain away the water. In a non-metallic bowl mix the mustard, chilli powder, sugar, salt, ginger and garlic to a smooth paste in the vinegar. Mix the vegetables thoroughly in the spiced vinegar and store in air-tight jars. Leave for 3–4 days before using. This pickle is delicious with cold meat.

Savoury Treats and Side-dishes

Pappadam

1 pkt pappadam (available at Indian grocery stores)
oil for deep frying

Using a pair of scissors cut each pappadam into four
equal sectors. Heat the oil until it is smoking hot. Put in
a pappadam. In a couple of seconds the pappadam will
expand and rise to the surface. Turn over and allow to
fry for two seconds. Drain on kitchen paper.

The frying should be done very quickly to prevent
pappadams from burning.

Pappadams are an ideal accompaniment to a curry
meal. They can be stored in an airtight tin for a few
days. There are several varieties of pappadams on the
market – the spiced ones are particularly delicious.
Allow about 4 pieces per person.

Samosas (Vegetable Pasties)   (Makes 30)

8 oz (226 gm) flour (plain)
2 tablespoonfuls melted ghee or oil
approximately 10 fl oz (284 ml) yoghurt
½ teaspoonful salt
oil for deep frying

Sieve the flour into a bowl and add the salt. Make a well in the centre of the flour and work in the ghee and sufficient yoghurt to form a stiff smooth dough. Leave covered in a cool place while the filling is made:

1 tablespoonful oil or ghee
1 onion finely chopped
¼ teaspoonful garam masala
¼ teaspoonful ground coriander
¼ teaspoonful ground cumin
½ teaspoonful salt
½ teaspoonful finely chopped ginger
8 oz (226 gm) mashed potato
4 oz (113 gm) cooked peas

Heat the oil and fry the onions until lightly browned. Add the spices and the rest of the ingredients and mix thoroughly. Allow the filling to cool.

On a dusted board roll out the pastry. Using a pastry cutter or glass 4 in. (10 cm) in diameter, cut out circles of pastry. Place a small quantity of the filling in the centre. Moisten the edges with cold water and seal. Using a table-fork press round the sealed edge to ensure that the pastry is well sealed. Repeat the rolling until all the pastry is used.

Heat the oil until it is smoking hot. Fry a few pasties at a time. Drain on kitchen paper and serve hot with chutney or ketchup.

Pakoda (Savoury Vegetable Fritters)

(Serves 6–8)

5 oz (142 gm) gram flour
1 teaspoonful salt
½ teaspoonful chilli powder
¼ teaspoonful ground turmeric
¼ teaspoonful baking powder
6 fl oz (170 ml) water
oil for deep frying

Sieve the gram flour into a bowl. Add the rest of the ingredients except the water. Gradually add the water to form a thick batter. Beat until smooth. The batter should be mixed just prior to use.

For this quantity of batter cut 1 potato, 2 onions and 2 green peppers into bite-sized pieces. Dip the vegetable pieces – a few at a time – and deep fry in smoking hot oil until golden brown. Alternatively finely shred 3 medium-sized onions and mix into the batter. Drop spoonfuls of the mixture into the hot oil and fry until golden brown. Serve hot with chutney or ketchup.

This is a wholesome snack which could be served with tea or as an accompaniment to a meal.

Patties (Savoury Pastries) (Makes about 50)

1 lb (454 gm) plain flour
1 teaspoonful baking powder
1½ teaspoonfuls salt
2 oz (56 gm) margarine
1 egg beaten
6–8 fl oz (170–226 ml) cold water
oil for deep frying

Sieve the flour and the baking powder into a bowl. Add
the salt. Rub in the margarine until the mixture resembles fine breadcrumbs. Make a well in the centre of
the flour and work in the beaten egg and sufficient
water to form a stiff dough. Mix thoroughly and leave in
a cool place for 30 minutes.

For the filling:

1 tablespoonful oil
1 onion finely chopped
⅛ teaspoonful ground turmeric
1 teaspoonful ground coriander
1 teaspoonful ground cumin
12 oz (340 gm) lean minced meat
1 teaspoonful chopped ginger
4 cloves garlic chopped
1 potato diced very finely
1 tomato chopped finely
¾ teaspoonful salt
1 oz (28 gm) creamed coconut dissolved in 2 fl oz (56 ml)
  hot water

Heat the oil and fry the onion until golden brown. Add
the spices, the meat and the ginger and garlic and fry on
a low heat for about 5 minutes. Add the potato, tomato,

salt and lastly the creamed coconut. Bring to the boil and cover and simmer for 20 minutes on a very low heat.

Since a dry curry is required, care should be taken to ensure that the meat does not stick to the pan by stirring the meat at regular intervals. Remove from heat and cool thoroughly.

On a dusted board or table roll out half the pastry to the thickness of fine pancake. Using a pastry cutter about 4 in. (10 cm) in diameter cut out rounds of pastry. Place a small quantity of the filling in the centre. Moisten the edges with cold water and seal. Using a table-fork press round the sealed edge to make sure that the patty is well sealed or else it will open during frying. Repeat the rolling until all the pastry is used.

Heat the oil until it is smoking hot. Put in about 5 patties at a time and fry until golden brown. Drain on kitchen paper and serve hot.

These savouries are very popular with drinks and are eaten at parties in Sri Lanka.

Khadi (Spiced Buttermilk)   (Serves 3–4)

15 fl oz (426 ml) natural yoghurt
5 fl oz (142 ml) water
½ teaspoonful sugar
½ teaspoonful salt
1½ tablespoonfuls gram flour
1 fl oz (28 ml) vegetable oil
½ teaspoonful cumin seed
few curry leaves if available
¼ teaspoonful ground turmeric
pinch of asafoetida (optional)

Blend the yoghurt with the water. Add the sugar and
salt. Make a paste of the gram flour with a little water.
Add it to the yoghurt mixture.

Heat the oil in a pan. When smoking hot add the
cumin seeds and put the lid of the pan on. Once the
seeds have stopped crackling add the curry leaves,
turmeric and asafoetida. Pour in the yoghurt mixture
and stir on a very low heat for 10 minutes. Garnish with
coriander leaves when available.

Serve hot in bowls or cups with lentil rice and
pappadam and pickle. This provides a gravy for the
vegetarian lentil rice. (See recipe on page 28.)

Mulligatawny (Spiced Beef Broth)

(Serves 4)

1 lb (454 gm) beef cut into small pieces
1 lb (454 gm) soup bones
2 medium-sized onions chopped
2 teaspoonfuls finely chopped fresh ginger
6 cloves garlic finely chopped
¼ teaspoonful ground turmeric
1 teaspoonful ground cumin
2 teaspoonfuls ground coriander
15 peppercorns
2–3 bay leaves
2 carrots diced
1½ teaspoonfuls salt
3 oz (85 gm) creamed coconut

In a large pan add all the ingredients except the creamed coconut. Cover generously with cold water and bring to the boil. Simmer on a *very* low heat for about 2 hours. Where a pressure cooker is available the cooking time of the stock is reduced to about 20 minutes. Strain the stock carefully saving the carrots, the onions and the pieces of meat.

In another pan heat a tablespoonful of oil and lightly brown a finely sliced onion. Add the stock and the meat etc. to the hot onion. Lastly add the creamed coconut and allow it to dissolve on a low heat in the soup. Prior to serving add a dash of lime or lemon juice (about 1 tablespoonful).

Serve hot either as a soup or as a gravy with boiled rice.

This is a South Indian and Sri Lankan speciality.

Egg Curry

6 eggs boiled and shelled
2 teaspoonfuls salt
¼ teaspoonful ground turmeric
3 fl oz (85 ml) vegetable oil
½ medium-sized onion chopped
2 cloves garlic chopped
¼ teaspoonful green ginger chopped
2-in. (5-cm) stick of cinnamon
1 dessertspoonful ground coriander
1 teaspoonful ground cumin
1 teaspoonful chilli powder
¼ teaspoonful ground fenugreek
1 oz (28 gm) creamed coconut
sprig of curry leaves (if available)
10 fl oz (284 ml) water
juice of half a lemon

Rub the eggs with salt and turmeric. Prick eggs with a pin and fry until brown. Heat 2 tablespoonfuls of oil and fry the onion until golden brown. Add the rest of the ingredients, except the eggs and the lemon juice, and simmer until the gravy is thick. Add the eggs and lemon juice and allow to simmer for a further 5 minutes.

This is an excellent dish for a vegetarian meal.

Omelette Curry

For the gravy:

2 fl oz (56 ml) vegetable oil
1 medium-sized onion chopped
½ teaspoonful chopped ginger
1 teaspoonful ground coriander
¼ teaspoonful ground fenugreek
1 teaspoonful ground cumin
½ teaspoonful chilli powder
sprig of curry leaves
1 teaspoonful salt
6 fl oz (170 ml) water
1 oz (28 gm) creamed coconut

To make the gravy heat oil in a pan and fry the onion until golden brown. Mix in all other ingredients except creamed coconut and water and cook, stirring continuously, for 5 minutes. Add water and creamed coconut. Bring to the boil and simmer on a low heat for 10 minutes.

For the omelettes:

6 eggs
½ medium-sized onion finely chopped
2 tomatoes chopped
1 green chilli finely chopped
2 teaspoonfuls salt
1 oz (28 gm) maldive fish (optional)
2 fl oz (56 ml) vegetable oil

Beat eggs and then add all other ingredients. Heat oil in a pan and make 3 large omelettes. Cut each omelette into 3 portions and add to the pan containing the gravy. Bring mixture to the boil and simmer on a low heat for 5 minutes.

This is an egg preparation that is peculiarly Sri Lankan.

Cheese Curry   (Serves 3)

40 fl oz (1·14 l) milk
juice of a large lemon

Bring the milk to the boil. Add the lemon juice to it. The milk will curdle and the cheese will separate from the whey. Pour through a muslin or a soft cloth and allow to drain. Squeeze out as much of the liquid as possible. The milk solids or cheese that are left in the cloth are then kneaded thoroughly. Divide into 5 portions. Shape each portion to form a cube. Deep fry the cubes of cheese until they are golden brown.

For the curry the ingredients required are:

2 tablespoonfuls oil
½ teaspoonful mustard seed
½ teaspoonful poppy seed
1 medium-sized onion finely chopped
1 medium-sized potato cut into small cubes
1 teaspoonful finely chopped fresh ginger
¼ teaspoonful ground cumin
1 teaspoonful ground coriander
½ teaspoonful garam masala
1 teaspoonful salt
1½ teaspoonfuls tomato puree
15 fl oz (426 ml) hot water
8 oz (226 gm) green peas

Heat the oil and allow the mustard seeds and poppy seeds to crackle. Add the onion and fry until golden brown. Fry the pieces of potato for a few minutes. Add the spices and fry for a minute. Add the rest of the ingredients including the cubes of cheese and bring to the boil. Cover and simmer for about 10 minutes.

This is an excellent vegetarian dish which can be eaten either with rice or chappatis.

Upama (Savoury Semolina) (Serves 4–6)

14 oz (395 gm) coarse semolina
1 tablespoonful oil
1 medium-sized onion finely chopped
½ teaspoonful cumin seeds
¼ teaspoonful ground turmeric
1 teaspoonful finely chopped ginger
a few curry leaves (optional)
2 green chillies (optional)
2 carrots grated
8 oz (226 gm) fresh or frozen peas
2 tomatoes skinned and chopped
1 teaspoonful salt
a knob of butter
a handful of cashew-nuts

In a heavy-bottomed pan roast the semolina. The roasting should be done on a low heat, stirring constantly to prevent the semolina from burning.

In another pan heat the oil and fry the onions until they are golden brown. Add the cumin seeds, turmeric, ginger, curry leaves and green chilli. Add the vegetables and 25 fl oz (710 ml) of water and bring to the boil. Lower the heat and allow to simmer for 10 minutes.

Add the roasted semolina and stir over the lowest possible heat for 3–5 minutes.

Remove from heat, cover and leave for 5 minutes. Add a knob of butter and cashew-nuts. Serve with pickle.

This is a South Indian breakfast dish but is equally nice eaten as a snack or with a curry for a main meal.

Lassi (Sweet Yoghurt Drink)

10 fl oz (284 ml) natural yoghurt
10 fl oz (284 ml) cold water
1 teaspoonful rosewater
sugar

Using an electric blender or egg beater, whisk the yoghurt and the water. Add the rosewater and sugar to taste. Pour into 4 glasses, add ice cubes and serve.

Iced Coffee

(Serves 6)

7 teaspoonfuls Nescafé (or other instant coffee)
40 fl oz (1·14 l) boiling water
7 fl oz (198 ml) sweetened condensed milk
1 tablespoonful sugar
1 teaspoonful vanilla esence
1 tablespoonful brandy (optional)

In a large coffee pot dissolve the coffee with the boiling water. Add the milk and sugar and stir until well mixed. Add flavourings and allow to cool. Chill in a refrigerator for at least 6 hours before serving.

A popular drink on a hot day – and very refreshing! A party beverage in Sri Lanka.

Desserts and Sweets

Yoghurt and Honey

In many homes in Sri Lanka yoghurt (made of buffalo milk) and treacle (from a palm) is the standard dessert. It is easy to make yoghurt in the home using milk and a small quantity of commercially made natural yoghurt. Boil 20 fl oz (568 ml) of milk and let it cool to blood heat. Add 1 oz (28 gm) of milk powder and 2 teaspoonfuls of yoghurt and stir until mixed. Put the milk in a bowl in a warm place for about 12 hours. An airing cupboard is ideal.

Jaggery Sauce   (Serves 4)

8 oz (226 gm) jaggery
10 fl oz (284 ml) water

Place the jaggery and the water in a heavy-bottomed pan. Cook over a very low heat until the jaggery has dissolved. Strain and cool before serving with yoghurt, banana fritters, pineapple fritters or ice-cream. This is a delicious sweet sauce and can be used as a substitute for a jam sauce.

Mango Ice-Cream

(Serves 6–8)

1 12-fl oz (340-ml) can evaporated milk
1 teaspoonful gelatine
3 oz (85 gm) castor sugar
1 12-fl oz (340-ml) can Alphonso mango pulp

Chill the evaporated milk in the freezer. In a small bowl soak the gelatine with a tablespoonful of cold water. Place the bowl in a pan containing hot water and over a low flame stir until dissolved. Using an egg beater or an electric mixer beat the evaporated milk until it is double in volume. Add the sugar and gelatine and beat again. Pour into a plastic container and chill in the freezer for 3–4 hours.

When the milk is frozen put it back into a bowl and beat thoroughly. Add the mango pulp and beat again. Pour back into the plastic container and freeze until stiff. This is delicious. Any fruit pulp can be substituted for the mango.

Mango Mousse

(Serves 6)

2 heaped teaspoonfuls gelatine
2 tablespoonfuls water
1 12-fl oz (340-ml) tin evaporated milk – chilled
2 tablespoonfuls sugar
1 1-lb (454-gm) tin mango pulp

Mix the gelatine in the cold water in a bowl and place over a pan of hot water. Make sure the gelatine dissolves thoroughly. Whisk the evaporated milk. Gradually add the sugar. Whisk in the gelatine. Fold in the mango pulp and set in a covered mould in the refrigerator for 3 hours. The mousse may be decorated with whipped cream and mango slices.

Srikhand (Sweetened Yoghurt Dessert)

(Serves 3)

40 fl oz (1.14 l) natural yoghurt
3 oz (85 gm) castor sugar
½ teaspoonful ground saffron
¼ teaspoonful ground cardamom
1 oz (28 gm) flaked almonds for garnishing

Pour the yoghurt into a fine muslin cloth and allow the whey to drain away by hanging the muslin over the sink for about 6 hours. Scrape the yoghurt solids into a bowl. Beat in the sugar either by hand with a wooden spoon or with an electric blender until the yoghurt mixture is smooth. Dissolve the saffron in 1 teaspoonful of hot water. Add the dissolved saffron and the ground cardamom. Garnish with the flaked almonds and serve well chilled.

Tropical Fruit Salad

(Serves 6)

A fruit salad made entirely or mainly with tropical fruit is a popular dessert in Sri Lanka. A typical combination would include pawpaw, mango, pineapple and banana. These fruits are peeled and diced, and mixed with lemon juice and sugar.

The availability of fresh tropical fruit is rather limited outside the tropics, but bananas are always available and pineapples are not uncommon. Many types of tropical fruit are available in canned form and can be used in a fruit salad.

1 medium-sized pineapple skinned, cored and diced
2 large bananas skinned and diced
1 can mango slices cut into small cubes
4 canned peach halves cut into small cubes
2 oranges peeled and divided into segments
juice of half a lemon
sugar to taste

Mix ingredients thoroughly and chill. Serve with ice-cream and chopped nuts.

Banana Fritters

4 oz (113 gm) plain flour
pinch of salt
1 tablespoonful icing sugar
8 tablespoonfuls lukewarm water
1 tablespoonful melted butter
whites of two eggs
6 bananas
oil for deep frying

Sift the flour and the salt into a bowl. Add the sugar and mix with the water and butter to a thick smooth batter. Whisk egg whites until stiff. Fold into the flour mixture. Peel and cut each banana lengthwise into two, and then each piece across its length into two.

Heat the oil until it is smoking hot. Coat each piece of banana in the batter and fry in the oil until golden brown. Drain on absorbent kitchen paper and serve hot with a jaggery sauce or any jam sauce.

Pineapple Fritters

Same as for banana fritters except use pineapple rings in place of banana quarters.

Watalappan   (Serves 4–6)

8 oz (226 gm) jaggery (available at Indian grocery stores)
7 oz (198 gm) creamed coconut
4 eggs
¼ teaspoonful grated nutmeg
½ teaspoonful grated lemon rind (optional)

Place the jaggery in a pan with 2 fl oz (56 ml) water. Boil
until the jaggery has dissolved. Strain and pour the
liquid jaggery back into the pan. Dissolve the creamed
coconut in the jaggery and allow to cool. Whisk the eggs
and pour into the milk mixture. Pour the mixture into a
bowl, add nutmeg and cover. Steam for 2 hours.
   Where jaggery is not available 8 oz (226 gm) dark
brown sugar may be substituted.

This is a traditional Sri Lankan dessert served for most
festive occasions.

Pineapple Surprise   (Serves 6)

8 oz (226 gm) cottage cheese
3 tablespoonfuls sugar
1 1-lb (454-gm) tin crushed pineapple
4 eggs
2 tablespoonfuls plain flour
1 teaspoonful vanilla essence
1 tablespoonful brandy (optional)

In a liquidizer blend the cottage cheese with the sugar.
Add the eggs one at a time and continue blending. Add
the rest of the ingredients and mix thoroughly. Pour
into a loaf tin and bake in a pan of water for 1¼ hours at

gas mark 3 (325° F). Allow to cool and then unmould.
Chill thoroughly before serving.

This is a light refreshing dessert.

Almond Pudding (Serves 6)

30 fl oz (852 ml) milk
3 oz (85 gm) ground almonds
4 oz (113 gm) milk powder
7 oz (198 gm) sugar
2 tablespoonfuls rosewater
¼ teaspoonful almond essence
sliced almonds for decoration

Boil the milk. Add the ground almonds and cook over a
low heat until the mixture thickens. Add the milk
powder a little at a time taking care to prevent the
formation of lumps. Add the sugar and cook over a low
heat, stirring all the time, until the mixture resembles
the consistency of a thick custard. Remove from heat
and add essences. Divide into 6 individual serving
dishes and decorate with sliced almonds.

Payasam

(Serves 4)

1 oz (28 gm) roasted vermicelli (available at Indian grocery
  stores)
1 oz (28 gm) butter or ghee
26 fl oz (738 ml) milk
2½ tablespoonfuls sugar
1 oz (28 gm) chopped blanched almonds
4 drops almond essence
¼ teaspoonful ground saffron
6 cardamoms

Break the vermicelli into 2-in. (2·5-cm) strands. Heat the
butter and gently fry the vermicelli until pale brown.
Add the milk and the sugar and bring to the boil. Lower
the heat and simmer for 20 minutes stirring at regular
intervals. When the mixture has thickened, add the
nuts, the essence, the saffron and the crushed
cardamom seeds. Cook for a further 3 minutes. Owing
to the fat content in the sweet it is best served at room
temperature.

Burfi

40 fl oz (1·14 l) milk
1 lemon
2 oz (56 gm) butter
2 oz (56 gm) milk powder
2 oz (56 gm) ground almonds
6 drops almond essence
castor sugar

Boil the milk. Add the juice of the lemon and boil for a
further 3 minutes. Strain in a muslin and allow the
whey to drip away. On a board dusted with icing sugar,

lightly knead the curds, butter, milk powder, the ground almonds and essence until the mixture is smooth. Weigh this mixture and add three-quarters its weight in castor sugar. Place in a pan and cook over a low heat for 20 minutes. Place on a buttered dish and cut into 12 1-inch (2·5-cm) squares.

Jalebis

(Serves 6)

6 oz (170 gm) plain flour
3 tablespoonfuls natural yoghurt
7½ fl oz (213 ml) water
½ teaspoonful ground saffron
1 lb (454 gm) sugar
20 fl oz (568 ml) water
20 fl oz (568 ml) oil

Mix the flour and the yoghurt. Gradually add the 7½ fl oz (213 ml) water and beat to a smooth batter. Add the saffron. Leave the batter covered in a warm place for about 10 hours.

Boil the sugar and water over a low heat and keep warm until the jalebis are fried. Heat the fat until smoking. Fill a funnel with the batter and pour spirals of the batter into the hot fat. When brown on both sides put into the sugar syrup. When they are soaked in the syrup place in a dish. Can be eaten hot or cold.

Rasagullas

40 fl oz (1·14 l) milk
juice of a lemon
1 lb (454 gm) sugar
40 fl oz (1·14 l) water
2 teaspoonfuls semolina
2 tablespoonfuls rosewater

Bring the milk to the boil. Add the lemon juice to it. The milk will curdle and the cheese will separate from the whey. Pour through a muslin or soft cloth and allow to drain. Squeeze out as much of the liquid as possible. Knead the milk solids or cheese that are left in the cloth thoroughly together with the semolina. Divide into 12 portions and form into small balls.

Boil the sugar and water in a pan. Once the sugar has dissolved and the syrup has been boiled for 5 minutes, divide the syrup into two. Allow half the quantity to cool and boil the rest. Once it is boiling add the cheese balls to the boiling sugar syrup and allow to continue boiling for 20 minutes. Remove the cheese balls and put into the cold syrup. Add the rosewater. Reheat on a low heat for 10 minutes before serving.

Gulab Jamun

(Serves 5)

1 oz (28 gm) butter
2 oz (56 gm) self-raising flour
4 oz (113 gm) full-cream milk powder
1 fl oz (28 ml) milk
oil or ghee for deep frying

for the syrup use:

8 oz (226 gm) sugar
20 fl oz (568 ml) water
1 tablespoonful rosewater

In a bowl mix the butter and flour to resemble fine breadcrumbs. Add the milk powder. Gradually work in the milk to form a stiff dough. Knead the dough thoroughly. Divide into 20 portions and form into balls.

Heat the oil or ghee and over a *very* low heat fry the gulab jamuns about 4 at a time. They will increase in size and gradually turn a dark brown colour. Drain on kitchen paper. If the gulab jamuns split during frying either the oil is too hot or the dough hasn't been kneaded sufficiently.

In a large pan place the sugar and water and bring rapidly to the boil. Reduce the heat and simmer for 5 minutes. Remove from the heat and allow to cool slightly. Add the rosewater and lastly the gulab jamuns.

Allow the gulab jamuns to soak in the syrup for a couple of hours before serving cold.

Semolina Pudding (Serves 3)

1 oz (28 gm) semolina
1 oz (28 gm) butter
15 fl oz (426 ml) milk
2 oz (56 gm) castor sugar
⅛ teaspoonful grated nutmeg
1 tablespoonful chopped cashew-nuts or almonds
1 tablespoonful sultanas
1 tablespoonful rosewater

Over a low heat fry the semolina in the butter for about 7 minutes. Add the milk and the sugar and stir continuously until thick (about 10 minutes). Remove from heat and add the rest of the ingredients. Pour into a serving dish.

This pudding can be eaten either hot or cold.

Almond Fudge
(Yields about 20 1-inch (2·5-cm) squares)

40 fl oz (1·14 l) milk
4 oz (113 gm) ground almonds
4 oz (113 gm) sugar
8 cardamoms ground
a few drops almond essence

In a heavy-bottomed pan boil the milk, stirring occasionally, until it is reduced to about 5 fl oz (142 ml). This should be done on a low heat to prevent the milk at the bottom of the pan from burning. Add the almonds and the sugar and continue to cook over a low flame, stirring continuously, until the mixture leaves the sides of the pan and begins to hold together. Remove from heat, add essences and pat down onto a well-greased dish.

Semolina and Coconut Rock

(Yields about 16)

8 oz (226 gm) sugar
2 fl oz (56 ml) water
5 oz (142 gm) semolina
1 oz (28 gm) coconut
1 fl oz (28 ml) rosewater
½ teaspoonful ground cardamom

Put the sugar and water into a pan and stir over a low heat until the syrup boils. Add the semolina and cook for about 5 minutes. Add the coconut, rosewater and cardamom and continue to stir until the mixture leaves the sides of the pan. Pour onto a well-buttered dish and cut into pieces.

Carrot Halva

(Serves 4)

3 oz (85 gm) butter or ghee
1 lb (454 gm) carrots finely grated
25 fl oz (710 ml) milk
5 heaped tablespoonfuls sugar
2 oz (56 gm) whole cashew-nuts or almonds
6 cardamoms crushed

Heat the butter. Add the carrots and sweat in the
butter. Pour in the milk, the sugar and the nuts. Cook
over a low heat, stirring occasionally, until the carrot
has absorbed all the liquid. (Approximately 40 minutes.)
Add the crushed cardamoms and serve at room
temperature.

Semolina Halva

(Makes about 24)

11 oz (311 gm) coarse semolina
4 oz (113 gm) butter or ghee
20 fl oz (568 ml) milk
7 tablespoonfuls sugar
2 oz (56 gm) blanched almonds
a few drops of almond essence
¼ teaspoonful ground saffron

Over a low heat, stirring continuously, roast the
semolina until pale brown. Add the butter, milk and
sugar and stir continuously to prevent the semolina
sticking to the pan. When quite stiff add the almonds,
the essence and the saffron which has been dissolved in
¼ teaspoonful of water. Mix thoroughly and pat onto a
buttered tray to a depth of about ¼ in. (6 mm). Cut into
1-in. (2·5-cm) squares.

Banana Halva

(Serves 3)

4 tablespoonfuls ghee
6 bananas peeled and sliced
8 oz (226 gm) sugar
1 teaspoonful ground cardamom

Heat half the ghee in a heavy-bottomed pan. Add the banana and stir continuously until the bananas become soft. Remove from the heat and mash the banana into a smooth pulp. Now add the sugar and the remaining ghee. Return to the heat and stir continuously until the mixture becomes a firm paste. Remove from heat and stir in the cardamom. Pour into dessert bowls and serve cold with a sprinkling of chopped nuts.

Milk Toffee-Fudge

(Yields about 24)

1 14-oz (396-gm) tin sweetened full-cream condensed milk
½ empty condensed milk tin of water
7 oz (198 gm) sugar
1 heaped teaspoonful cocoa powder dissolved in
  ½ teaspoonful hot water
2 oz (56 gm) butter
2 oz (56 gm) chopped cashew-nuts

Place the milk, water and sugar in a heavy-bottomed pan. Cook over a low heat for about 35 minutes. Add the cocoa, butter and nuts and cook for a further 5 minutes. Remove from heat and pat down onto a well buttered dish. Cut into 1-in. (2·5-cm) squares while warm.

Potato Toffee

(Yields about 25)

1 lb (454 gm) potatoes
1¼ lb (567 gm) sugar
4 fl oz (113 ml) water
3 cardamom pods
1 tablespoonful rosewater

Wash and boil the potatoes. Peel away the skin and mash thoroughly. In a heavy-bottomed pan mix the sugar and the water and slowly bring to the boil. When the sugar has dissolved add the mashed potatoes and cook over a low heat, stirring constantly, for about 45 minutes or until the mixture leaves the sides of the pan. Crush the cardamom seeds and add them together with the rose-water to the toffee mixture. Spread thinly on a buttered plate and cut into 1-in. (2·5-cm) squares.

Sesame Sweets

(Yields about 16)

6 oz (170 gm) brown sugar
2 fl oz (56 ml) water
4 oz (113 gm) sesame seeds

Put the sugar and water in a pan and over a low heat stir until the sugar dissolves. When the sugar is syrupy add the sesame seeds and stir continuously over a low heat for about 4 minutes. Pour onto a buttered dish and while warm cut into squares.

Masur Pak

(Makes 16 pieces)

3 oz (85 gm) ghee
4 oz (113 gm) sugar
4 fl oz (113 ml) water
1½ tablespoonfuls gram flour
1½ tablespoonfuls ground almonds
6 cardamom pods
sliced almonds for decoration

Place the fat, sugar and water in a pan. Bring to the boil
and allow to cook for 5 minutes. Reduce the heat and
into this sizzling mixture gradually beat the sieved flour.
Care should be taken thoroughly to mix each addition of
flour. Add the ground almonds and lastly the crushed
cardamom seeds. Stir for about 7 minutes on a low heat
until the mixture leaves the sides of the pan. Spread on a
dish and decorate with almonds.

This is an oily rich sweet.

Coconut Cake

(Serves 6)

4 eggs
8 oz (226 gm) castor sugar
8 oz (226 gm) desiccated coconut
4 oz (113 gm) ground rice
2 fl oz (56 ml) rosewater
4 oz (113 gm) chopped cashew-nuts
⅛ teaspoonful ground cardamom
¼ teaspoonful ground cinnamon
pinch of ground cloves

Whisk the egg yolks and the sugar until thick and
creamy. Add the coconut and fold in the ground rice.
Add the rosewater and the spices and nuts. Whisk egg

whites until stiff and fold into the cake mixture. Pour
into 2 greased cake tins and bake at gas mark 3 (320° F)
in the centre of the oven for 45 minutes.

This cake has a crusty top with a moist interior.

Love Cake

8 oz (226 gm) butter
8 oz (226 gm) semolina
10 egg yolks
1 lb (454 gm) soft brown sugar
1 teaspoonful grated nutmeg
1 teaspoonful grated lemon rind
½ teaspoonful ground cinnamon
1 tablespoonful rosewater
2 teaspoonfuls vanilla essence
1 tablespoonful honey
12 oz (340 gm) cashew-nuts minced or finely chopped
4 egg whites whisked

Soften the butter and gradually mix in the semolina.
Leave in a warm place so that the semolina is soaked
into the butter. Cream the egg yolks and gradually beat
in the sugar until light and creamy. Add the spices,
rosewater, vanilla and honey. Beat in the semolina and
butter. Add the nuts and lastly fold in the whites of the
eggs. Pour into a lined rectangular cake pan (12 in. ×
12 in. – 30 cm × 30 cm) and bake at gas mark 1 (280° F)
for 2–2½ hours or until done. Cut into squares before
serving.

This is an unusual spicy cake with a nutty flavour and
can be stored in an airtight container for about a month.

This is a speciality of Sri Lanka, a recipe reputed to have
been handed down by the Dutch.

Coconut Rock

5 oz (142 gm) sugar
2 fl oz (56 ml) water
4 oz (113 gm) desiccated coconut
3 drops of food colouring (optional)
2–3 drops vanilla essence

Put the sugar and the water in a pan and cook over a low heat until the sugar has dissolved. Add the coconut and stir over a low heat for about 10 minutes or until the mixture leaves the sides of the pan. Add the colouring and essence and pat down onto a well-buttered dish. Shape into a square and cut into 1-in. (2·5-cm) pieces.

This is a popular sweet with children.

Menu Suggestions

Indian and Sri Lankan food is ideal for dinner parties, offering a wide range of interesting and delectable menu combinations. I shall list here a few of my favourite menus but the possible total number of combinations is, of course, legion. Curry dishes have the added advantage for parties in that they can be prepared in advance, to be heated in the oven or on the stove just before serving. Wine is not usually served with meals, but this is mainly due to the lack of suitable wines in India and Sri Lanka. There is no reason why you should not serve a good bubbly white wine or a claret with a meal, or even an iced lager or cider.

The number of dishes that go to make a curry meal in India and Sri Lanka is usually dependent on the state of affluence of the particular household. At the humbler extreme there would be just a rice dish, a lentil curry and perhaps a green vegetable that together suffice to serve a basic nutritional need. At the other extreme a meal could consist of well nigh a dozen separate dishes. In planning a curry meal here in the West it would be sufficient to include for the main course a meat dish, a vegetable dish and a lentil dish together with a rice or bread preparation. It is usual to accompany a curry meal with a selection of pickles, chutneys and pappadams. The main course could be followed by either yoghurt, fruit or one of the many desserts I have included in my recipes.

137

Main course combinations

Menu 1

Yellow Rice
Chicken or Prawn Curry
Aubergines
Spiced Fried Potatoes
Pappadams
Pickles and Chutneys

Menu 2

Chicken Biriani
Seeni Sambol
Egg Curry
Curried Fried Bhindi
Cucumber Raita
Date Chutney

Menu 3

Vegetable Pilaf
Deep-Fried Karella
Lentil Curry
Prawn Curry
Pappadams

Menu 4

Rice
Shikh Kebabs
Mushroom Curry
Onion Salad
Pappadams

Menu 5

Savoury Rice Sticks
Spicy Pork
Mālu Cutlis
Date Chutney

Menu 6

Nan
Tandouri Chicken
Onion Salad
Potato and Pea Curry
Assorted Pickles

Menu 7

Paratha
Cauliflower Bhaji
Black-eyed Beans
Beef Curry

Menu 8

Rice
Lentil Curry
Beef Curry
Leeks and White Cabbage
Coconut Chutney (2)
Pappadams

Menu 9

Lentil Rice
Stuffed Cauliflower
Khadi
Lemon Pickle
Pappadams

Menu 10

Rice
Cheese Curry
Mixed Salad
Tomato Chutney
Pappadams

Menu 11

Chappatis
Moong Dhal with Spinach
Boti Kebabs
Onion Salad

Menu 12

Vegetable Pilaf
Stuffed Bhindi
Omelette Curry
Fish Rissoles
Pappadams

Menu 13

Rice
Lentil Curry
Fish Curry
Stir-fried Spinach
Pappadams

Menu 14

Puris
Rice
Chick Peas
Chicken Curry
Spiced Green Beans
Mixed Salad

Menu 15

Savoury Rice Sticks
Chicken Curry
Mulligatawny
Coconut Sambol
Cucumber Salad

Menu 16

Rice
Cheese Curry
Chappatis
Avial
Lettuce with Peanut
    Dressing

Menu 17

Paratha
Chick Peas
Courgettes
Keema Curry
Date Chutney

Menu 18

Rice
Mackerel in Tamarind
Pumpkin Curry
Lentils (1)
Coconut Chutney (2)

Menu 19

Pilaf Rice
Kashmiri Lamb with
    Dried Fruit
Aubergines
Mint Chutney
Pappadams

Appendix

Oven Temperature Conversions

	Gas Mark	Degrees Fahrenheit	Degrees Centigrade
Very Slow	¼–½	240–280	115–135
Slow	1–2	280–320	135–160
Warm	3	320–340	160–170
Moderate	4	340–370	170–185
Fairly hot	5–6	370–400	185–205
Hot	7	400–440	205–225
Very hot	8–9	440–480	225–250

Index

Entries in *italics* do not refer to recipes

Allspice, 13
Almond Fudge, 128
Almond Pudding, 123
Aniseed, 13
Asafoetida, 13
Aubergines, 11, 79
  Fried, 79
Avial (Mixed Vegetables in
    Yoghurt Sauce), 81

Baby Marrow (*see*
    Courgettes)
Banana:
  Fritters, 121
  Halva, 131
Beans:
  Black-eyed, 74
  Spiced Green, 74
Beef Curry, 39
Beefbroth, Spiced (*see*
    Mulligatawny)
Bhindi, 11
  Curried Fried (Okra or
    Lady's Fingers), 80
  Stuffed, 80

Biriani:
  Chicken, 31–2
  Vegetable, 27
Bitter Gourd (*see* Karella)
Black-eyed Beans, 74
Boti Kebabs, 60
Bread Dishes, 34–8
  Chappatis, 34
  Nan (Leavened Bread),
    36
  Paratha, 37
  Puri, 35
  Roti, 38
Broccoli, Stir-fried (*see*
    Spinach Stir-fried)
Broken Orange Pekoe Tea,
    23–4
Burfi, 124
Buttermilk, Spiced (*see*
    Khadi)

Cabbage:
  and Split Peas, 70
  Leeks and White
    Cabbage, 71

Spring Cabbage, Stir-
    fried (*see* Spinach,
    Stir-fried)
  with Coconut, 70
Cakes:
  Coconut, 133
  Love, 134
Capsicum, 14
Caraway, 14
Cardamon, 9, 14
Carrot:
  Halva, 130
  Sambol, 94
Cauliflower:
  Bhaji, 67
  Stuffed, 68
Cashew-nut Curry, 83
Cayenne Pepper, 14
Ceylon Tea, 23–4
Chana Dhal, 89
Chappatis, 34
Cheese Curry, 112
Chick Peas, 88
Chicken:
  and Lentil Curry, 49
  Biriani, 31–2
  Curry (1), 43–4
  Curry (2), 44
  Curry (3), 45
  Kashmiri-style, 46
  Korma, 47
  Spicy Fried, 48
  Tandouri, 50
  with Dried Fruit, 49
Chilli, 9, 14
Chutney:
  Coconut (1), 97

Coconut (2), 98
Date, 96
Serving of, 19–20
Tomato, 96
Cinnamon, 9, 15
Clarified Butter (*see* Ghee)
Cloves, 9, 15
Coconut, 10
  Cabbage with, 70
  Cake, 133
  Chutney (1), 97
  Chutney (2), 98
  Cream of Coconut, 10
  Desiccated, 10
  Milk Rice (Yellow Rice),
    29
  Products: Toddy,
    Jaggery, Arrack, 10,
    16
  Rock (Sweet), 135
  Semolina and Coconut
    Rock, 129
  White Radish with, 78
Coconut Sweets:
  Coconut Cake, 133
  Coconut Rock, 135
  Semolina and Coconut
    Rock, 129
Coffee:
  Iced, 115
Coriander, 9, 15
Coriander Leaves, 15
  for garnishing, 19
Courgettes, 76
Crab Curry, 65
Cucumber Raita, 94
Cumin, 15

Curried Fried Bhindi (*see* Bhindi)
Curried Meat Balls, 41
Curried Stuffed Peppers, 82–3
Curry Leaves, 15
Curry Powder, 9
  Recipes for Mixes, 21–3

Date Chutney, 96
Deep-fried Karella (Bitter Gourd), 68
Desserts and Sweets, 117 *et seq*
Dhal:
  Recipes for, 89–92
  Various Types of, 11
Dosa (Lentil Pancakes), 92
Dried Fish, 11
Dried Fruit with Chicken (*see* Kashmiri Lamb with Dried Fruit)
Dried Fruit with Lamb (*see* Kashmiri Lamb with Dried Fruit)
Dried Green Peas, 69
Dried Prawn Sambol, 95

Earthenware pots, 19
Egg:
  Curry, 110
  Omelette Curry, 111–12

Fennel, 15
Fenugreek, 16
Fish:
  Curry, 62

Mackerel in Tamarind, 62–3
  Rissoles (Mālu Cutlis), 60–1
  in Yoghurt Sauce, 61
Friccadels (Crisp-fried Meat Balls), 42
Fruit Salad, Tropical, 120
Fudge:
  Almond, 128
  Milk Toffee, 131

Garam Masala, 16
  Recipes for Mixes, 21–3
Garnishes, 19
Ghee, or Clarified Butter, 23
Ginger, 16
Goa, Speciality of, 53
Gram Flour, 11
  Leeks in, 72
Green Beans, Spiced, 74
Gulab Jamun, 127

Halva:
  Banana, 131
  Carrot, 130
  Semolina, 130

Ice Cream, Mango, 118
Iced Coffee, 115
India, 7 *et seq*

Jaggery, 10, 16
  Sauce, 117
Jalebis, 125

Karella (Bitter Gourd), 11
    Deep-fried, 68
Kashmiri Lamb, 56
    with Dried Fruit, 57
Kashmiri Specialities:
    Chicken, Kashmiri-
        style, 46
    Kashmiri Lamb, 56
    Kashmiri Lamb with
        Dried Fruit, 57
Kebabs, 58
    Boti, 60
    Shikh (1), 58–9
    Shikh (2), 59
Keema Curry, 40
Khadi (Spiced Buttermilk),
    108
Kofta, Nargisi, 42

Lady's Fingers (see Bhindi)
Lamb:
    Kashmiri, 56
    Kashmiri Lamb with
        Dried Fruit, 57
    Spicy Lamb Curry, 55
    in Yoghurt, 54
Lassi (Sweet Yoghurt
    Drink), 114
Leeks:
    and White Cabbage, 71
    in Gram Flour, 72
Lemon Pickle, 99–100
Lentil, 11
Lentil Dishes:
    Chana Dhal, 89
    Chicken and Lentil
        Curry, 49

Dosa (Lentil Pancakes),
    92
Lentil Rice, 28
Lentil Rissoles (Vadés),
    89–90
Lentils (1), 86
Lentils (2), 87
Moong Dhal with
    Spinach, 90
Thur Dhal, 91
Lettuce with Peanut
    Dressing, 93–4
Liver Curry, 51
Love Cake, 134

Mace, 16
Mackerel in Tamarind, 62–3
Main Course Combina-
    tions, 138 et seq
Maldive Fish, 16
Mālu Cutlis (Fish Rissoles),
    60–1
Mango:
    Ice Cream, 118
    Mousse, 118
Marrow:
    Courgettes, 76
    Spicy Marrow, 76–7
Masur Pak, 133
Meat Balls:
    Curried, 41
    Crisp-fried (Friccadels),
        42
Meat, Poultry and Fish
    Recipes, 39 et seq
Menu Suggestions, 137 et
    seq

Milk Sweets:
  Almond Fudge, 128
  Almond Pudding, 123
  Burfi, 124
  Gulab Jamun, 127
  Milk Toffee-Fudge, 131
  Payasam, 124
  Rasagullas, 126
  Semolina Pudding, 128
Milk Toffee-Fudge, 131
Mint Sambol, 95
Mixed Pickle, 100–101
Mixed Vegetables in
    Yoghurt Sauce
    (Avial), 81
Moong Dhal with Spinach,
  90
Mousse, Mango, 118
Mulligatawny (Spiced Beef
    Broth), 109
Mushroom Curry, 77
Mustard Seed, 17

Nan (Unleavened Bread),
  36
Nargisi Kofta, 42
Nutmeg, 9, 17
Nuts, chopped for
    garnishing, 19

Okra (see Bhindi)
Omelette Curry, 111–12
Onion Salad, 93
Onions, for garnishing, 19

Pakoda, 105
Pappadam, 103

Paratha, 37
Patties (Savoury Pastries),
  106–7
Payasam, 124
Peanut Dressing, Lettuce
  with, 93
Peas:
  Cabbage and Split Peas,
    70
  Chick Peas, 88
  Dried Green Peas, 69
  Potato and Pea Curry,
    73–4
Pepper, 17
Peppers, Curried Stuffed,
  82–3
Pickle:
  Lemon, 99–100
  Mixed, 100–101
Pickles, serving of, 20
Pilaf:
  Rice, 25–6
  Vegetable, 26
Pineapple Fritters, 121
Pineapple Surprise, 122–3
Poppy Seeds, 17
Pork:
  Spicy (with Liver), 52
  Vindaloo, 53
Potato:
  Curry, 72–3
  and Pea Curry, 73–4
  Spicy Fried, 85
  Toffee, 132
Prawn:
  Curry, 63
  Dried Prawn Sambol,

(*Dried Prawn Cont'd*)
  95–6
  and Tomato Curry, 64
Pumpkin Curry, 84
Puri, 35
Radish:
  White Radish with
    Coconut, 78
Raita (*see* Cucumber Raita)
Rasagullas, 126
Rice, 9
  Basmati, 9
  Boiled, 25
  Long Grain Patna, 9
Rice Dishes, 25 *et seq*
  Chicken Biriani, 31–2
  Coconut Milk Rice
    (Yellow Rice), 29
  Lentil Rice, 28
  Pilaf Rice, 25–6
  Plain Boiled, 25
  Spicy Risotto, 30
  Sweet Rice, 33
  Vegetable Biriani, 27
  Vegetable Pilaf, 26
Rice Sticks, Savoury
    (String Hopper
    Pulao), 32–3
Risotto, Spicy, 30
Rissoles:
  Fish (Mālu Cutlis), 60
  Lentil (Vadé), 89–90
Roti, 38

Saffron, 17
Salads:
  Onion, 93

Lettuce with Peanut
    Dressing, 93–4
Salads and Chutneys, 93 *et
    seq*
Sambol:
  Carrot, 94
  Dried Prawn, 95–6
  Mint, 95
  Seeni (Spiced Onion),
    98–9
Samosas (Vegetable
    Pasties), 103–4
Savoury Pastries (Patties),
    106–7
Savoury Rice Sticks (String
    Hopper Pulao), 32–3
Savoury Semolina (*see*
    Upama)
Savoury Treats and Side-
    dishes, 103 *et seq*
Savoury Vegetable Fritters
    (*see* Pakoda)

Vegetables and Lentils, 67
    et seq
Vegetables Mixed in
    Yoghurt Sauce, 81
Vermicelli Milk Dessert
    (Payasam), 124
Vindaloo, Pork, 53

Watalappan, 122
White Cabbage:
  Leeks and, 71
White Radish, 11
  with Coconut, 78

Yellow Rice, 29
Yoghurt:
  Avial (Mixed Vegetables
    in Yoghurt Sauce), 81
  Fish in Yoghurt Sauce, 61
  and Honey, 117
  Lamb in Yoghurt, 54
  Lassi (Sweet Yoghurt
    Drink), 114
  Srikhand (Sweetened
    Yoghurt Dessert), 119
Yoghurt Desserts:
  Srikhand, 119
  Yoghurt and Honey, 117

Zucchini (*see* Courgettes)

Notes

Notes

Notes

Notes

Notes

Notes

Notes

Notes

Notes

Notes

OTHER COOKERY BOOKS FROM CORONET

DELIA SMITH

☐	16876 5	How To Cheat At Cooking	95p
☐	21002 8	Frugal Food	95p
☐	23094 0	Evening Standard Cookbook	95p
☐	22158 5	Book of Cakes	£1.25

CAROLINE LIDDELL

☐	25454 8	The Wholefoods Cookbook	£1.50

IRFAN ORGA

☐	25074 7	Cooking With Yoghurt	£1.25

RUBINSTEIN AND BUSH

☐	23837 2	Ices Galore	85p

All these books are available at your local bookshop or newsagent, or can be ordered direct from the publisher. Just tick the titles you want and fill in the form below.

Prices and availability subject to change without notice.

CORONET BOOKS, P.O. Box 11, Falmouth, Cornwall.

Please send cheque or postal order, and allow the following for postage and packing:

U.K. – 40p for one book, plus 18p for the second book, and 13p for each additional book ordered up to a £1.49 maximum.

B.F.P.O. and EIRE – 40p for the first book, plus 18p for the second book, and 13p per copy for the next 7 books, 7p per book thereafter.

OTHER OVERSEAS CUSTOMERS – 60p for the first book, plus 18p per copy for each additional book.

Name ....

Address ....

....